PROBLEMS OF INDIAN DEFENCE

PROBLEMS OF INDIAN DEFENCE

K.M. PANIKKAR

GYAN

Published by

GYAN

Gyan Publishing House
5, Ansari Road
Daryaganj, New Delhi-110002
Phone: 011-47034999, 9811692060
E-mail: books@gyanbooks.com

Distribution Network
gyanbooks.com
India, USA, Canada, UK, Australia

ISBN: 978-93-7225-007-7 (PB)

First Published, 1960

2nd Impression 2025

Printed at: Gyan Press, Delhi.

PROBLEMS OF INDIAN DEFENCE
Author: K.M. PANIKKAR

PROBLEMS OF INDIAN DEFENCE

PROBLEMS OF INDIAN DEFENCE

K. M. PANIKKAR

CONTENTS

INTRODUCTION

" WHEN WHOLE nations are the armies and the science of destruction vies in intellectual refinement with the science of production I see that war becomes almost impossible from its own monstrosity ": so said William James over fifty years ago. Though the conditions postulated have undoubtedly arisen and it may even be said that the science of destruction more than vies in intellectual refinement with the science of production, war has by no means become impossible from its own monstrosity. True, the logical conclusion of scientific warfare is each other's total destruction by nuclear weapons. This, however, is not very much of a possibility now, since a balance of power has been achieved between the two most powerful nations possessing nuclear weapons. Others like England and France will soon reach the same position. So a nuclear war may be said to have become in William James' phrase " impossible from its own monstrosity ". But that does not exclude war with conventional weapons helped no doubt by new processes based on nuclear energy. For example, we know already that nuclear-powered submarines, which could remain submerged for long periods, are already under construction. Again inter-continental ballistic missiles, even if they do not carry nuclear war-heads, have so enlarged the range of warfare as to revolutionize it altogether. While therefore a total nuclear war may be ruled out altogether, the idea that limited wars would also cease, and we shall for ever more live in an atmosphere of peace, would seem to be no more than wishful thinking. The strategy of war would no doubt undergo radical changes. The changed nature of weapons will undoubtedly lead to new tactical conceptions and important organizational changes. But the objectives of defence would not be seriously changed for defence is legitimate resistance to force applied to gain the objectives of a policy detrimental to the defending state. This objective has never changed any more than the object of offensive warfare which is to force the enemy to yield to demands which the state considers to be important for the achievement of its policy. The idea that the object of war is the destruction of the enemy's forces, as Clausewitz states in a famous passage, is only half true for the real object of war is to achieve a peace which secures the objects one has in view such as territorial acquisition and the weakening of the economic and political position of the enemy. Sometimes these objects could be achieved without ever fighting a battle. Similarly, the best defence often is to foil the enemy's plans against one's own security or interests without ever striking a blow. Such a position can arise only when the policy of a state is directed with wisdom and foresight and the military organization to meet any enemy attack is known to be adequate. Security of a country can be ensured only if two conditions are satisfied : first, if its policy is guided with an appreciation of its permanent security interests and secondly, if its defence forces are organized in a manner capable either alone or with the help of its allies of withstanding all attack. This means in the first place that the foreign policy of a country must be based on an awareness of power relationships and must at all times be directed to the primary object of ensuring the security of its borders and — now when subversion has become a major weapon of offensive action — the safeguarding of its internal security also.

It would be trite to say that defence today has to be total, in the same way that warfare has become total; that is, it is not merely a question of having an excellent military organization, but a firm social structure which could stand the strain of external pressure, and an economic structure which could not only keep a modern army in the field supplied with the latest equipment, but could at the same time meet essential civilian requirements. Agriculture, industry, transport of all kinds, become as much a part of defence activity as military action in the field when every section of life is open to attack from the air. With the disappearance of the borderline between the front and the rear in warfare, the defence of essential productive capacity, both agricultural and industrial, has become one of the vital aspects of war effort. In fact it may well be said that the rear services play a decisive role in defence. This means that the armed forces depend not only on the production and supply of necessary armament, but also on the intricate and subtle relations between the public and the armed forces, on the firmness of the country's social integration, the willingness of the general public to suffer sacrifices and work and on the soundness of its economy. Without the support of the people behind the lines, no army could fight. Today when the line of division has practically ceased, the rear as providing the bases, the direction and the resources plays a decisive role.

Consequently, defence can no longer be considered a matter solely for the armed forces. Not only is every section of the community interested but has become an active participant in defence. The success of defence will consequently depend as much on the civil leadership of the homefront, as on the military leadership of the battlefront, as much in the way in which the homefront holds against enemy attacks, both direct and subversive, as the firmness with which the battlefront is held.

The present study deals only with the general aspects of the problem of India's defence. It makes no attempt to deal with the organization and equipment of the armed forces and other technical aspects of defence. That is a matter for professional soldiers with adequate knowledge of the development of weapons, their performance, the organization suitable for new weapon-schemes, etc. This is true not only of the army, but equally of the navy and air force. Though this aspect of the question has been generally left out in this work, I consider it necessary to discuss in general terms three aspects of the problem because of the widespread public interest in them.

The first is: what kind of an army is it that India requires for defence purposes? There is a demand in India in certain quarters for the introduction of conscription. The arguments usually advanced are three. First it is said that India has for long been disarmed and had to live under foreign authority, and consequently large sections of people have now no tradition of military activity. They have, the argument runs, become physically "soft" and they lack stamina and endurance. This, it is said, is dangerous to the nation and it is argued that it is only through compulsory military service that a sense of discipline and physical toughness can be cultivated on a national scale, so that the softness of the "mild" Hindu will disappear.

Secondly, it is held that the obligation to defend the country should be equally shared by all. The risks, the dangers and the responsibilities should be distributed evenly and not be placed on particular communities or groups of people. A modern army, it is claimed, is a nation in arms and no one should be excluded and no one allowed to exclude himself from the duty of defending the motherland.

A third argument is that it is dangerous to political liberty to depend solely on a standing army or on military forces recruited only from certain communities for the defence of the country.

It is necessary to examine these arguments carefully. It is true that during the period of British rule in India many areas and communities were classified as non-martial and excluded from recruitment to the army. It is equally true that many of these groups have become lacking in physical endurance and stamina. It may also be conceded that it is a matter of the highest national interest to revive physical sturdiness and other qualities which these communities have lost. But conscription is hardly the way to do it. Apart from the enormous cost involved in introducing compulsory national service in a country of over four hundred million, it will be playing with our army in a dangerous way and weakening it. There are many ways in which the non-martial classes could be brought forward and effectively incorporated in the defence system. Recruitment of suitable men from among them should be encouraged. The factors that stood in the way of their taking an active interest in the army should be removed. They should be encouraged to join para military organizations: territorial formations, cadet corps and volunteer formations and other auxiliary forces. But to conscript them in order to make them military-minded would appear to be the most ineffective way of making them martial.

The second argument about the equal obligation of all to defend the country and to share equally in the risk has an appearance of greater validity than the first. But that also would hardly stand up to examination. In present day warfare the uniformed soldier fighting in the front represents only one aspect of war. Undoubtedly he is in many ways the most important. But the labourer in the factory and the tiller in the field, workers on the railways and other transport services, the staff in the agencies of communication, telegraph, wireless, radar, etc., are no less important for national defence. If the soldier is trained to fight, disciplined and organized in units, the workers in steel plants, armament factories, shipbuilding yards are also highly skilled. Since those in essential civil employment are also sharing, along with the soldiers at the front, the responsibility of defence the argument of equal sharing of burden loses much of its weight.

It is used to be held that while work in the factory or on railway trains is undoubtedly important the risk to life in the case of the soldier at the front puts him in a special category. This is undoubtedly true though in the age of missiles and air bombardment the dangers on the homefront have also increased beyond any previous experience. In the case of Hiroshima and Nagasaki the danger to the civilian population was infinitely greater within a limited period of time than anything which might happen when two armies are locked in battle. In the circumstances, the argument that conscription distributes the danger more or less equally has also lost much of its ground.

The danger to public liberties from standing armies is a belief which has a respectable antiquity. The history of the praetorian guards in Rome and of the Janissaries in the latter days of the Ottoman empire are outstanding instances of dangers to the stability of the state itself arising from the powers of the army. In England the fear of the standing army as a support to autocratic royal power was so deeply rooted that constitutionally speaking the sanction for the military establishment is annually renewed by Parliament. Recent events in Asian and African countries, Thailand, Pakistan, Egypt, the Sudan and elsewhere have emphasized this danger, more especially in states where democracy is new and has not taken deep root. But would this danger be avoided by conscription? Conscription does not do away with a permanent military nucleus of all arms, land army, navy and air force. What it does is to train all people of different age groups, who could then be called up at short notice, thus making it possible for the army to include all able bodied men when necessary. In a country like India, compulsory national service would mean training for thirty-five or forty million people, in itself a task of almost inconceivable magnitude — useless for military purposes and utterly wasteful from the point of view of finance and resources.

What India needs for her defence is an army with long-term service, not too large but highly trained and equipped with the latest and most effective weapons. This regular army should be capable of being extended rapidly when occasion arises both in terms of manpower and of officers — through organizations functioning in peacetime, cadet corps, territorials and volunteers. If she has an army of 350,000 men and a proportionately strong navy and air force, trained and equipped to the highest standards, her own purposes of defence would be more than amply served provided the army is backed by organizations like the national cadet corps and territorial forces which would enable it to be expanded at will at a time of crisis.

It is not a quantitative army that we require but a qualitative one built around the most powerful weapon system available. When weapon power was weak generally, numbers counted over everything else. That period may be said to have represented the handicraft period in industry. But today warfare is more like automation, powerful, accurate and with self-operative machines with trained personnel in control. I am not talking here of nuclear warfare, I.C.B.M.'s, etc. but of warfare with what are today known as conventional weapons. So, for the purposes of Indian defence what is required is a compact mechanized army, highly trained and equipped with the most powerful weapon system available. Its organization has to be in terms of the problems it is called on to tackle, the terrain it has to fight on, the enemy it has to meet and the climate and other conditions in which it has to function.

Another point of importance in respect of modern defence forces is the necessity to have a unity of command. Till the first Great War the problem was not particularly important. So far as England was concerned, there was really speaking only one service, the navy, whose overwhelming strength protected the interests of the British Empire and secured the safety of her positions. Similarly, continental powers did not greatly count on the sea though Germany was building up her strength and France had a navy of considerable power in the Mediterranean. Warfare for the continental states meant battles between land armies, while for Britain it meant the enforcement of her authority on the seven seas. The situation changed with the first Great War. Great Britain was compelled to become a land power, a situation from which she has not been able to revert to her original position, as a result of the revival of German power and later of the Soviets. What complicated the situation further was the growth of an air arm whose importance rapidly increased with time. Three services meant three separate commands and, worse, inevitable rivalries.

Though the division into different services was unavoidable at the beginning when land army's operations were not so dependent on the other arms as they became during the course of the second World War, today this division though organizationally important has ceased to count from the point of view of strategy. The separation of the three services under independent commands is indeed an outmoded concept. A division of functions makes sense, as Kessington points out, only if functions represent distinguishable strategic missions. Today, this is not possible. The services have from the point of view of strategy to work in unison. Without adequate air support ground forces today are ineffective, without ground forces the air force can only undertake predatory operations. Airborne operations involve both equally. The separation of functions and the independence of the three arms have thus ceased to be an orthodox doctrine. With the British the pre-eminence of the navy and with the French and the Germans the primacy of the army were previously unquestioned. But today even in the citadel of orthodoxy, the British Admiralty, the principle of the unity of command is accepted. So far as India is concerned, under the British, armed forces meant only ground forces. It is only after India's freedom that the question of the independence of the other services has arisen as a serious issue, and fortunately the unity of the political control of the defence forces under a Defence Minister enables a unity of command to be developed without serious difficulty.

The defence of a country is primarily the safeguarding of its territorial integrity from outside attack. Today, however, the situation has an extended meaning as it also involves the maintenance of the integrity of a country from subversive attacks under inspiration or even direction from outside. Events all over the world have shown that the security of a country may be imperilled without a single foreign soldier setting his foot on its soil. Such has no doubt been the case in former times also when internal rebellions were promoted by the agents of external powers. Kautilya considers this not only legitimate but a necessary measure in the case of unfriendly countries. In recent years internal subversion through fifth column activities has again assumed the status of a major tactic in war. Primarily it is not the function of the defence forces to deal with internal subversion unless it amounts to a revolt and becomes a civil war. But a consideration of the problem of a menace to the social and political structure of a country, meant to bring that country under the political control of a foreign power, is unavoidable in any discussion of defence in modern times.

How is a country to deal with subversion which aims not merely at changing a government but at weakening it in relation to a foreign power? Clearly unless it develops into a civil war, which postulates a division in the armed forces themselves, it is impossible to use against one's own country the more powerful weapons in its defence armoury. Bombardment from sea, bombing from air, leave alone any organized military campaign, is obviously out of question. How then is a country to be defended from such conspiracies against its independence? Though this is essentially a matter of internal security, not connected directly with armed forces, it has an important bearing on the action of the army. No army can function effectively if its homefront is not firmly held and if the country as a whole does not give the fullest support to its armed forces. The fifth column in wartime is in fact no less than a camouflaged civil war meant both to weaken national morale, and to make the armed forces feel that they are unsupported from behind. Consequently it is essentially a problem of defence in its widest sense.

The question of dealing with such subversive activities and generally of maintaining the internal solidarity of the nation is unconnected with defence organization in democratic countries and is the function of civil governments. It is the normal work of the police and the Home Ministry, and defence organization comes into it only when attempts are made to tamper with the loyalty of the armed forces or where such activities trench on the intelligence activities of the forces or their secrets.

This aspect of the question is not therefore dealt with in the present work.

CHAPTER I

INDIAN MILITARY TRADITION

THE MOST important of all the factors which led to the failure of Indian defence at the end of the twelfth century, leading to the conquest of North India by the Muslims, and later to the conquest of India by Britain during the period of Moghul breakdown, was her failure to develop a theory of war and defence. From the earliest days, as even the *Vedas* bear witness, bloody wars were fought on the soil of India by parties contending for territorial authority. Some of the battles such as the Battle of the Ten Kings described in the *Rig Veda*, and that of Kurukshetra, around which the epic of *Mahabharata* was written, were indeed of far-reaching consequences, decisive in many respects to the development of Indian history. But even these celebrated battles and others of which we have knowledge prove to us two indisputable facts. The battle was not between regular armies trained in warfare but between tribes under their tribal leaders or between champions representing the two sides. Also, though the warriors were accoutred in mail and rode chariots, and used many effective weapons, there is no evidence that the simple principle that men formed into a unit, supporting mutually and functioning as a unit, are many times stronger than mere numbers, a principle on which all scientific warfare developed, was even known to them.

Indian armies till the time of the Muslim invasions consisted of trained war elephants, a formidable and almost invincible weapon in those days, warriors in horse drawn chariots, and masses of infantry carrying every kind of weapon but with no effective training or discipline. The warriors were highly trained in the use of weapons, but the soldiery consisted mainly of peasants impressed at the time and provided with arms. Even kings who maintained standing armies paid no attention to their training, grouping or discipline. In the fighting among Indian powers this system did no particular harm, as it would appear war was not with the Hindu monarchs a serious occupation. Every ruler was supposed to go on campaigns of conquest after Dasserah, mainly to overawe feudatories, to put down recalcitrant nobles and, if conditions permitted, to enlarge his own territory by defeating his neighbours. The rules of war were strict. The cultivators, women and cattle were not to be disturbed. Monarchies were not without adequate cause to be uprooted but only reduced to vassalage, and an enemy who offered tribute was not to be molested.

In battle the elephant did most of the havoc as the weapons available at the time were ineffective against that animal if properly protected against arrows by mail. The reputation of Indian war elephants was so great that Seluccus obtained from India 300 of them and it was by their use that he won his great battle against Philedelphus, for the Asian heritage of Alexander. So long as the pre-eminence of the elephant remained and the horse was used in war mainly for drawing chariots, Indian military methods were adequate for India's own defence. In fact no conqueror may be said to have set foot in the Gangetic valley as long as the pre-eminence of the war elephant remained unchallenged. The Persians for a time occupied the Indus region which was known to them as India. It was this territory that Alexander conquered, and the kings that he claimed to have defeated were but petty chieftains living under the protection of the Persian satrap. From the middle of the Punjab, Alexander retreated to Persia. Nor did other invaders at any time before Mohammed Ghori in 1194 effectively conquer the Gangetic valley. The Sakas, the Huns and other predatory tribes tried but vainly to break through to the Gangetic valley but the Indian defence system stood firm against all invaders. But the situation was undergoing a change to the disadvantage of India. The invention of the stirrup by the Central Asian nomads produced a revolution in military strategy comparable to the invention of the internal combustion engine in our own times. Before the stirrup was invented the horse was mainly used for drawing chariots in war or for transporting the warrior. It gave the rider great mobility. But it was not as effective as the elephant for the rider of the elephant could shoot his arrows from his seat on the elephant or throw his javelin and other weapons. With the coming of the stirrup the situation was entirely changed. The rider on the horse was thus able, with his feet firmly in the stirrup, to stand up while riding and shoot his arrow. This was decisive. From the time the stirrup came into wide use, the cavalry became the major weapon of offence, incomparable, till the development of the internal combustion engine, in speed, manoeuvrability and capacity to go anywhere and at the same time to work in formation.

The Hindus, it is significant to emphasize, developed no cavalry of their own till the rise of the Mahrattas. The superiority of the Muslims in Indian wars was the mastery of the horse which they inherited with the Central Asian traditions. Irvine, the historian of the Moghul army, emphasizes the fact that cavalry was the main arm on which the Moghuls depended for their victories. The

Hindu armies, based mainly on ponderous elephants and numerous but untrained infantry, broke before the cavalry charge of the Turki and later Moghul invaders. The heroism of individual warriors and the training of elephants were of no avail.

The Muslim armies which held the Gangetic valley, Malwa and Bengal under them and raided the kingdoms of South India under Allauddin Khilji consisted mainly of cavalry. For lightning raids over long distances this was the ideal arm. With the Moghuls a new factor enters the scene. Babar who rode to Delhi with 25,000 men had brought with him some pieces of artillery, which is the first appearance of cannon in land warfare in India. Just a quarter of a century earlier Vasco da Gama had arrived at Calicut and the ship which brought him also carried cannon. Cabral had bombarded Calicut with it at the beginning of the century. But in land warfare the first to use cannon in India was Babar. It was his artillery that gave the Moghul invader his victory over Rana Sanga.

With the introduction of these two arms — cavalry and cannon — warfare may be said to have entered a new stage in India. But it is significant that no military tradition developed in India even under the Moghuls. Infantry under the Moghuls was not trained, or organized, or equipped as a serious arm of warfare. They were not organized in regiments or trained to fight in formation. Orme, the historian, noted that the infantry of the Moghuls consisted of " a multitude of people assembled together without reference to rank or file : some with swords and targets who could never stand the shock of a body of horses ; some bearing matchlocks which in the best of order can produce but a very uncertain fire ; some armed with lances too long or too weak to be of any service even if ranged with the utmost regularity of discipline."

The soldiers were neither recruited nor trained nor paid by the state. They were got together by commanders who received a fixed sum for every man. They were mostly levies collected by petty zamindars or belonging to jungle tribes forcibly brought for this work. The commander collected the money and kept the men as a retinue. For overawing local population they were important but in the field they were more of a handicap. Bernier who was a competent observer estimated that around the emperor, in the capital, there were no more than 13,000 infantry, including musketeers, foot artillery and generally every person connected with artillery. With no training and no discipline the infantry was in fact of no great importance as became only too evident when the Moghul armies came into conflict with better disciplined forces.

Not only was the infantry untrained, inefficient and not properly organized in regiments, but the artillery, which gave the Moghuls their victory against the Rajputs was hardly better. Babar had brought with him technicians capable of founding cannon and in his memoirs records the founding of one at Agra under the direction of Ustad Quli Khan. But unfortunately his successors did not make any progress in the work and most of the heavy cannon cast in the Moghul times was under the direction of foreign experts. Also, the management of artillery had not been well mastered. Orme in his *Military Transactions* notes that the Carnatic army "having never experienced the effect of field forces had no conception that it was possible to fire with execution the same piece of cannon five or six times a minute; for in the awkward management of their own clumsy artillery they think they do well if they fire once in a quarter of an hour."

The artillery that the Moghuls had was effective so far as the " country " powers were concerned. It enabled Akbar to conquer Hindustan and his immediate successors to hold it; but against foreign troops equipped with field guns the Moghul artillery was altogether ineffective. Also the Moghul artillery was too heavy. The pieces could only be transported with difficulty and kept in position by extraordinary measures. They were mounted on bundles of bamboos tied together and each piece was drawn by twenty or thirty pairs of oxen.

It is also to be noted that there was never any system of drill or training in any wing of the armed forces. As was to be expected from the Moghuls with their Central Asian traditions, the cavalry men excelled in horsemanship but it was an individual achievement and not so much a training in formation. The infantry, recruited as it was by a leader, was organized around him. If they were musketeers they knew the use of muskets; others to wield their spears, swords or battle axes according to the weapons they carried. There was no uniformity of weapons. Though great attention was paid to the development of the body, there was no collective training and therefore the army was at all times more a mob than an organized force.

The battles which these armies fought were more a series of skirmishes than actual battles of formation. True, the Moghuls arranged their field in the manner prescribed in Taimur's Ordinances. The skirmishers were in front. Behind them was a line of artillery with supporting columns, on either side. The commander-in-chief took his position in the centre and to the right and left there were reserves which could be thrown into the battle. Behind the commander-in-chief was the rear guard. Actually, though the armies were arranged in this formal fashion, once the battle started it had a tendency to become converted into a series of skirmishes. Victory was decided not by superior strategy or tactics but by numbers.

It was clear to early European observers that a smaller force, trained and disciplined to fight in formation, could defeat the unorganized masses which constituted the armies of Indian rulers. It is this knowledge that led Dupleix, and following him the English East India Company, to organize the sepoy army. The secret of the sepoy army was simple. Organized and trained in the way that European soldiers were the Indian soldiers would be cheaper, better suited and perhaps not less efficient than European soldiers in the circumstances of India. A hundred years of warfare from the time of Clive's intervention to the second Sikh war proved this beyond doubt. The sepoy army was the instrument with which the East India Company conquered India.

Three characteristics marked out the sepoy army from the armed forces of Indian rulers before the middle of the eighteenth century. They were drilled, disciplined and trained in the use of arms. Secondly, they were organized in units, battalions, regiments and brigades and the units functioned in peacetime cantonments and in war under their own officers. Thirdly, as they were regularly paid, housed in cantonments and their comforts looked after, they were made to feel contented. In fact the sepoy army was modelled on European military systems. There was one major difference. The sepoy army had two sets of officers, a set of Indian officers with ranks like *Jamedar*, *Subedar*, *Risaldar*, *Subedar Major*, *Risaldar Major*, similar to those in use in the armies of Indian princes, who served as intermediaries between the commissioned European officers and the rank and file, and the command was in the hands of European officers. The Indian officers were men from better-class families and held commissioned ranks but they went up only to a rank equivalent to that of a Major. The European officer corps constituted the real leadership of the sepoy armies.

The Indian officer cadre had only what may be called training in drill and in the use of arms. They were ignorant of tactics and strategy, without a knowledge of which they could not replace the Europeans. This was clearly demonstrated in the history of the great rebellion of 1857–58. The regiments that mutinied received no effective leadership from their officers. They marched in formation and made a good show, but when it came to battles, their leadership failed them. The sepoy army had in fact no knowledge of warfare, no leadership of its own, and was therefore able to fight wars only under the leadership of European officers.

The Indian rulers of the time were not slow to realize the importance of the military revolution of which the rise of the sepoy army was the proof. They began to organize their own troops in the same manner and to build up considerable forces under European leadership. The armies that Haidar Ali built up with the assistance of the French, the Nizam under the command of Raymond, Mahadaji Scindia under de Boigne and Perron and, above all, Ranjit Singh under Avitabile, show how widely the consequence of this revolution was recognized and was sought to be adopted.

In fact, the second half of the eighteenth century may be considered as a critical period in the development of India's military thinking. It was during that period that the untrained hosts of Indian rulers were gradually transformed into trained armies with adequate cavalry and artillery support. The regiments that de Boigne organized, though they were scattered at Assaye and Laswari, were formidable forces compared to the armies of other Indian rulers. It is with them that Mahadaji Scindia established and maintained his authority over North India. The regiments that Avitabile raised for Ranjit Singh held their own in the Sikh war against the East India Company, and the war against the Sikhs included some of the most hard fought battles in India.

The main weakness of the forces raised and trained by the Indian rulers in the latter half of the eighteenth century was the lack of a properly trained officer cadre. Even in the Moghul army there was no system of graded officers and there seems to have been no course of training for officers. It is true that in the Mahratta army of Shivaji, where a system of direct recruitment was tried, there was an officer cadre selected and appointed by the commander-in-chief. Of the cavalry officers the lowest in rank was the *havaldar*. He commanded a unit of twenty-five horsemen ; over five such units was placed a *jumladar*, while a *hazari* had under him ten *mumlas*. Over him was the *panch hazari*, who served directly under the *sarnobat* or the commander-in-chief. But the system that Shivaji founded did not survive him as under Raja Ram the army again became feudal, and the officers in due course became attached to hereditary fiefs.

Besides, though the Indian rulers imitated the organization of the Company's armies, they were unable, generally speaking, to understand either the strategy or the tactics of large-scale warfare. So far as the East India Company was concerned it was provided with the officer corps that was recruited from England. Among the Indian leaders of the eighteenth century no one, except Haidar Ali, an untutored genius, understood strategy and effectively used Western tactics in battle.

The essential point is, however, that without an educated officer corps which studied warfare as a science, understood all aspects of it, paid attention to the battles of the past and strategy of the great leaders, the creation of a modern army capable of meeting a well-trained force in battle is altogether impossible. For great geniuses like Ganghiz Khan and Taimur previous training may not have been necessary. But geniuses apart, it is only by careful and prolonged training of officers that an army could be made an effective instrument of warfare. This is what the Indian armies of the eighteenth century lacked. They were organized and equipped like the armies of the East India Company. Their men were trained in a similar manner. But they had no effective corps of officers educated in warfare.

During the period of British rule (1818–1947) the organization, training and equipment of the Indian army continued to improve. Indians, however, were excluded from the officer class of the army till after the first Great War so that leadership was exclusively British. After the first Great War the principle was gradually modified and though to the very end the Indian officers continued to be a small minority of the whole, they were sufficient in number to provide the nucleus of a new leadership for the army.

Thus, India had till independence lacked an effective military tradition. She had developed no doctrines of warfare with a corpus of theory, no effective inherited organization, no knowledge of the progress of warfare in other countries. India in fact did not have an effective system of defence. The human material was superb. From the point of view of courage, endurance, ability to act with discipline and self-control, the Indian armies trained by Britain have proved themselves to be second to none. But neither under the British, nor under Indian rule was there developed in India a proper military tradition based on the experience of warfare in other countries or with a coherent and effective doctrine of its own.

CHAPTER II

GROWTH OF THE MODERN INDIAN DEFENCE SYSTEM

AN INTEGRATED conception of the defence of India, and a doctrine of Indian defence supported by a consistent foreign policy are among the two major contributions of Britain to the Indian people. Britain conceived the defence of India as a continental system. It was the strategic area around the Indian subcontinent that became the centre of Britain's interest in safeguarding the territorial integrity of India. Any threat to India's borders from anywhere, Britain planned to meet halfway, unlike the Indian rulers of Delhi who fought their major battles at Panipat far in the interior of India.

As early as the first decade of the nineteenth century, when Britain's interest had become dominant in the Indo-Gangetic valley, she sent a mission under Sir John Malcolm to the court of Persia to explore the possibilities of an alliance with the Shah's empire in order to meet the threat of a combined Franco-Russian invasion of India which had been discussed at Tilsit by Emperor Napoleon and Czar Alexander. However fantastic the scheme might appear now, the danger at the time seemed serious enough. What is significant is not so much that the two emperors should have thought of attacking British power in India, but that a conception of Indian defence based on the Persian Gulf and in agreement with the Shah's empire should have emerged from that crisis.

Since that time, till the end of the British rule in India, the Persian Gulf was an area of strategic interest for Britain. The interest of course varied with circumstances. As long as the Turks were the allies of Britain, the issue lay dormant. But when the Berlin-Baghdad railway came to be mooted and imperial Germany in alliance with Turkey began to show her interest in these areas, the reaction of the British Government was decisive. The British Indian Government strengthened its agreements with the rulers of strategic areas in the Trucial Coast and made it clear to the world that any attempt to interfere with its position in the Persian Gulf would be an act of hostility.

The interest in Afghanistan, though originally expansionist, became during the second half of the nineteenth century a matter of Indian defence. When Lord Lytton intervened in the affairs of Afghanistan it was in the hope, as he himself stated, of "bequeathing to India the supremacy of Central Asia and the revenue of a first class power". In his imagination Lord Lytton saw the vision of an Indian empire stretching deep into Central Asia. In a letter to Lord Cranbrook he pleaded for "an opportunity of disintegrating and breaking up Kabul power". But the disastrous consequence of his Afghan adventure made his successors withdraw from this too forward a position and limit themselves to the safeguarding of India's defence by erecting Afghanistan into a buffer state.

What gave urgency to this problem and changed the character of British relations with Afghanistan from one of clear aggression to a policy of friendly neutralization was the rapid advance of the Russian empire into Central Asia. "Russia on the Oxus is Russia on the Ganges", exclaimed an English statesman in the House of Commons. Though the distance between the two rivers is considerable, and the fear may be considered exaggerated, the idea behind the declaration is clear enough. The presence of a great military power on the Oxus meant a threat to British power in India if the intermediate area remained a vacuum. Britain could no longer afford to think in terms of reducing Afghanistan to the position of a feudatory state, as Lytton had dreamed earlier. Nor could she afford to alienate the Afghans. The erection of the Afghan kingdom as a friendly buffer state was thus decided upon in the interest of Indian defence.

In Sinkiang and Tibet Britain followed similar policies. Even here, it was not any fear of aggression from China against which Britain was trying to safeguard her Indian frontiers. The eternal bogey was the Russian bear. Dorjieff's alleged intrigues with the Russian court gave a seemingly valid excuse to the Tibetan adventure, while so far as Sinkiang was concerned Russia's actual presence in the Pamirs and near Alma Alta was sufficient to awaken Britain's awareness of the Russian position in relation to India. France's presence in Indo-China and her gradual approach to the Burmese frontier awakened Britain's memories of Anglo-French rivalries on the Indian peninsula. Though the intervention in Burma was mainly based on economic considerations, the possibility of the French acquiring a foothold at the Mandalay court and thereby creating a new frontier for India on the north-east was not outside the calculations of the Indian Government.

Lastly, there was the question of the defence of India from the sea. For Britain the question of India's naval defence did not arise till the end of the first Great War. She was till then the unchallenged mistress of the seas and her predominance in the sphere was overwhelming. The design of imperial Germany to outflank the sea power by the Berlin-Baghdad Railway had been successfully checkmated, as also the desire of imperial Russia to reach out to the warm waters of the Indian Ocean. For a long time there was no problem, therefore, of naval defence so far as India was concerned.

But the period following the first World War witnessed a notable change in the situation. The Washington Conference on the limitation of naval strength clearly showed that the days of Britain's unchallenged supremacy on the seas had passed. It was only then that Britain awoke to the necessity of building a regional navy based on India which would in time grow up as a powerful subsidiary of the Royal Navy. Thus the Indian navy came into existence more as a symbolic force than as an arm capable of defending India's coastline. By the time of the second Great War the navy had expanded into an effective though small regional force and in this capacity it played a notable part. The growth of the Indian navy in the period of the war is thus described in a speech by Admiral Fitzherbert, then Commander-in-Chief of the Indian navy.

"With regard to the expansion of ships, he produced a construction programme by means of which every shipbuilding slip in India was filled; when a ship slipped down into the sea the keel was laid for the next. He had very great cooperation from shipbuilding experts and others who overcame all difficulties. The problems were new, but they shouldered the burden, and he was very grateful to them all. Ships were built in India, Australia, the United Kingdom and the United States, and gradually they came into service, and when the plan was complete there would be not five, but 250 modern ships in the Royal Indian Navy. Recruits were being enlisted at the rate of thousand a month, so that his 23,000 would now be nearing the 30,000 mark.

Two major naval bases had been built and three minor bases fitted with the needs of a modern minor naval base, so that attention had not only been given to ships and men, but also to the housing problem."

Thus at the end of the British rule, India had a powerful and developed army, a small but efficient navy and a nucleus of an air force. It was the army that constituted India's main defensive strength, as in the other two arms British India could depend upon the strength of Britain's own fleet and air force.

The army itself was peculiarly constituted. It consisted of two parts, a British army in India and the Indian army proper, and it was only when the two were combined that it made a major instrument of war. After the Mutiny (1857–58) the British, with accustomed political wisdom, quietly reorganized the Indian army so that it became ineffective as a striking force without the active cooperation of the British army in India.

Also, a second feature of the Indian army was its class composition. It was recruited from what the British termed the martial classes, Pathans, Baluchis, Punjabi Muslims, Jats, Sikhs, Garwhalis and other special castes and communities. Whatever the motive, it created a gulf between the army and the people, especially as the British Government took the greatest care to keep these communities, broadly speaking, uncontaminated by the rising spirit of nationalism.

The Indian army was in that sense not national; it had been converted into a special interest. In the (unofficial) Commonwealth Conferences in London as late as 1945, the representative of one of the martial classes even put forward the claim that in any political changes that might be introduced in India, the disproportionate representation which his small community possessed in the army should not be affected. For all its courage, devotion and discipline, the Indian army under the British had become, especially in its latter days, an instrument of sectionalism in internal politics.

There were two other factors in respect of the Indian army which require to be emphasized. In the first place, it was an instrument of imperial policy and not merely an army for the defence of India. Apart from the expansionist campaigns in Afghanistan and Burma which Britain undertook with the Indian army as its main instrument, it became in the second half of the nineteenth century the force on which Britain's imperial system in Asia was based. Britain's power radiated from India to different parts of Asia and some parts of Africa (Somaliland). The Indian army showed its colours in Peking during the Boxer Rebellion, paraded the streets of Shanghai in times of trouble, marched up to Lhasa, fought in Somaliland. In fact it was, before the first World War, almost the sole instrument of Britain's imperial policy in the East.

The Indian empire itself was organized as a continental system, a regional power stretching out its arms into Central Asia, to the Arabian coast, and to the Far East. Apart from the British navy, the force on which this great imperial system was built was the Indian army. The Indian empire, that extraordinary organization which though subordinate to Whitehall carried on within its own range an imperial policy, played a strange and important part in the politics of Asia on the basis of its armed might available for action at short notice anywhere.

This remarkable instrument of imperial policy fashioned in India out of Indian manpower was, till the end of the first World War, entirely officered and led by British personnel. No Indian was entitled to receive a

King's Commission in that army. A few cadets were recruited at the end of the war. After the first Great War, with the political changes that were then introduced, a cautious programme of limited Indianization of army leadership was undertaken. It was this group of officers originally trained at Sandhurst who took over the army command from the British in 1947.

Secondly, it was also an army of occupation through which the British Government imposed its will on the Indian people. The Indian army was therefore not popular with the masses of the Indian people, except of course with the sections from which it was recruited. The British authorities encouraged to a certain extent these differences. The educated classes were always held up to the army as *babus* and *banias*, with whom the loyal elements should not associate. The nationalists, on the other hand, looked upon the army with suspicion, branding it as a mercenary force without any sense of national or patriotic feeling.

The accusation that the Indian army was composed of mercenaries was on the whole unjust. As the recruitment was confined to certain classes, a broad hereditary relationship had come to exist between these classes and the army leading to a sense of loyalty and attachment. The Indian army had been recruited from the same areas and from the same group for over a hundred years. Consequently, generations had grown up attached to the army, looking upon it as their normal career and feeling it as an honour and an opportunity.

After the First War a subtle change came over all this. With the rise of an integral nationalism in India, the situation underwent a radical change. It should be remembered that the first outburst of new nationalism was in that paradise of military orthodoxy, the Punjab, where Muslims, Sikhs and Hindus joined together in the days immediately following the Great War. The Akali movement affected the Sikhs of all classes. The Khilafat agitation to which the Congress had also given support stirred the Muslim masses. The Mahatma's emergence as the national leader at the head of the non-cooperation movement had repercussions even on classes which had so far stood outside the national struggle. The British Government was alive to the dangers of the situation and it was obvious that the old policy of completely isolating the martial classes could no longer be sustained especially when, with the Montagu-Chelmsford reforms, responsible government was accepted as the objective of Indian policy.

A policy of gradual Indianization of the officers' ranks of the army was therefore unavoidable. It is well to remember that it was Mr. Jinnah, then a leading champion of nationalism, who was the strongest advocate of Indianization of the army leadership. He served on the committee which the Government of India appointed to make recommendations on this question and the modest proposal of gradually officering eight regiments with Indians, trained in time in India, arose out of the committee's proposals.

The original training at Sandhurst was a wise move as otherwise it might have created two different castes in the Indian army and stamped the Indian officers with the stigma of inferior training. But it was obvious that when the number of cadets increased, India would have to develop her own Defence Academy. The Indian Military Academy at Dehra Dun, which was established to meet this demand and was a modern and up-to-date institution modelled on Sandhurst, for the first time provided India with facilities for training officers for the army.

When this limited scheme was put into effect one significant fact which was noticed was that the young men who came forward for training belonged to the more advanced classes of society and were not limited to what Britain had designated as the martial classes. It was these officers who played their part in the second Great War and gained sufficient experience to take over the army from British commanders.

The defence organization as evolved by the British authorities in India, though modified to a degree by the admission of a small number of Indians in the ranks of officers, had not undergone any basic change for nearly a hundred years. It had, of course, kept pace with developments elsewhere in respect of armament, organization and training, but that was in consequence of its dependence on Britain.

The significant fact about the Indian army was that it was not an independent force. Its control was from London. Its training, equipment and employment were determined by the general staff in England. This subordinate character of the Indian army affected it in many ways. It had no independent policy in regard to armament. Though there were ordnance factories in India, and equipment of different kinds were manufactured in the country, for the more complicated arms and heavier equipment the army was dependent on British industries. There was of course no organization for research in arms or equipment, or even an industrial potential capable of supporting the army in time of war. Even with regard to the railways, telegraphs and other means of communications, the essential material, e.g. locomotives etc. for railways, equipment for telegraph lines, had to come from England.

In short the Indian army under the British was not the independent arm of a nation-state, but an instrument which in the hands of an industrially advanced power could be used for its imperial purposes. The second World War proved this conclusively. The Indian army in the early days of the war, when Britain's sea power was threatened and all her resources had to be concentrated in Europe, was left without proper equipment. The army was not adequately mechanized. The resources for such mechanization had not been developed in India. There was neither adequate air defence for the country, nor air support to the army. It was only after America came into the war that the Indian theatre came to be organized adequately to undertake a campaign on its own.

The partition of India led, of course, to the partition of the army, the dividing up of not merely the units but the equipment, material and other stores which go to make up an army. As the Muslim officers mostly opted for Pakistan, and the units which had a Muslim majority were allotted to the new state the army may be said to have been split up even more than the civil services. The staff college at Quetta being in Pakistan fell to that state. Actually it is a marvel that the army survived this cruel operation and emerged out of the ordeal as the national defence forces of India and Pakistan.

CHAPTER III

THE DEFENCE PROBLEMS OF FREE INDIA

THE PROBLEM that India faced after partition was to reconstitute the defence forces on a new basis. The mechanical regrouping of the army as a result of partition had been carefully worked out and was carried through with smoothness and efficiency.

Out of the old Indian army, two national armies were then born. But though the units were regrouped and the stores and equipment divided, the Indian army (no doubt the Pakistan army also) faced many major problems to which much attention had not been given in the past. These could be briefly stated as involving the transformation of the Indian army to an independent national force, adequately trained and equipped to meet unaided threats to the nation's integrity.

The Indian army was, as we saw, supplemented by the British army in India, and it was only the combined force that provided adequate defence for the country. The British army in India had naturally to be withdrawn. The Indian army had, therefore, to take over the functions previously fulfilled by the British units. This meant a considerable increase in the strength of the armed forces, with the consequent necessity for increase in facilities for training and schools for specialized courses. Secondly, the Indian army could no longer go on with its traditions of martial and non-martial races. Every effort had to be made to give the armed forces a national complexion without, however, giving rise to a feeling of discontent among the privileged classes of the past. A reserve of officers and men had to be created and the entire country made to feel the direct responsibility for defence.

Besides these political aspects of defence organization it was obvious from the beginning that the lessons of the Great Wars had to be digested and incorporated in the formation and training of India's new armies. That was no easy matter. Indian army leadership during the war had been exclusively British. No Indian had risen above the rank of a Brigadier. Also, the experience of warfare in the jungles of Burma was different from the experience in the deserts of Africa or in the Appennines.

The immense effort which the Allies put into the Western Front and the Russians on the Eastern Front had its own lessons which were not fully known to anyone in India. A modern army must draw from the experience of all. If the Indian army was to be something more than a second class force meant only for internal security, then its training and organization had to be based on the latest knowledge. It was impossible without adequate cooperation from one of the major powers to acquire this knowledge. Close association with Britain was for India the only practical alternative and India chose it unhesitatingly.

There were many reasons why an association with Britain was preferred to cooperation with any other country. The organization, traditions and disciplining of the Indian army had been built up by the British and were to a large extent modelled on the British army. The officer-private relations, the mess life, the *esprit de corps* of the units and the structure of command were all on the British model. Arms and equipment were also to a large extent similar.

In the circumstances cooperation at higher levels was easier. There was also the question of language. For these and other reasons India decided to continue her association with Britain in the higher fields of defence organization and for the regular training of selected service officers at the Imperial Defence College. She had also the advantage of participating in the conference of general staff officers and in other ways of taking full advantage of the membership of the Commonwealth to build up her own army.

Before she could even give serious thought to the problem of reorganizing her army, events in Kashmir forced her hands to give to defence problems the attention which she might not otherwise have given. Within two months after India's independence, the princely state of Jammu and Kashmir was subjected to an organized invasion from outside. The Maharaja's forces melted away and at the last moment in November 1947 the Maharaja appealed to India to come to his aid.

In order to enable India to defend his territory, the Maharaja signed the instrument of accession to the Union of India and thus made it a part of Indian territory. To defend Kashmir from the raiders became thus an obligation of India. This task which was entrusted to the army was no easy one.

Kashmir was connected with the rest of India only by one road which was snowbound at the Banihal Pass and could not be crossed either on foot or on vehicles in winter. Also, in the plains the road was too near the Pakistan boundary which enabled the raiders, who were freely making use of Pakistan territory, to attack the convoys. The Indian air force had but few transport planes. In fact, the organization of the operation which was to save Kashmir from the invaders was beset with difficulties that would have strained the skill of the most experienced general staff.

This was not all. By almost a superhuman effort, the army units with necessary equipment were transported to Kashmir. But the conditions of fighting were unusual there. Winter in Kashmir is particularly severe, and to the Indian units, most of which came from the plains, the conditions of warfare must have been exceptionally hard and yet the units of the Indian army which were rushed to Kashmir in November 1947 threw the invaders out of the valley even after the regular Pakistan forces had come to the raiders' support. For the last twelve years the Indian army has kept vigil over the Pir Panjal ranges and the high Himalayan peaks safeguarding the territory of the Union and keeping Kashmir safe from attack.

It is only the discipline, training and sense of national interests that enabled the Indian army in the difficult conditions of the winter of 1947–48 to do this wonderful work. Its consequences have been also remarkable. Overnight, so to say, the Indian army became popular with the public. During the British period, the general public had looked upon the army with suspicion. There was never any enthusiasm for its achievements. But the campaign in Kashmir changed all that. Since November 1947, when the army first intervened in Kashmir, there has never been any criticism of expenditure incurred for the better equipment and training of the army or any feeling except one of pride in the nation's attitude towards the defence forces.

The Kashmir experience has another important aspect. For the first time in modern times Indian forces fought under the overall command of Indian officers. Ever since the Indian army had been organized it had always been under the command of European officers at all levels till the modest scheme of Indianization in the late twenties of this century. But the officers who had been recruited had not become senior enough during the second Great War to have command in battle over units larger than regiments. Even those were only a few. The Indian army was in fact taken over by a group of young officers who, whatever their merits and however great their enthusiasm, were practically without experience of higher command either in peace or in war. The campaign in Kashmir was the first serious experience of fighting on their own initiative, when they had to plan, organize and execute field operations.

The experience was invaluable for the new army and its officers. It gave them self-confidence. It also enabled them to understand the real problems behind campaigns which no amount of manoeuvres would have taught them. The public of India also was pleasantly surprised and felt grateful to the army. That the army had, under the most trying conditions upheld the honour of India, cleared the valley of invaders and saved Kashmir for India, made the common man in India look upon the army with respectful admiration.

Also, the Kashmir experience made the army authorities themselves realize some of the major gaps in their training. The Indian army had not a single alpine unit capable of functioning effectively in snow-clad mountains and at high altitudes. Its air transport was below requirements. It is only battle experience that enables army authorities to see these weaknesses. From all these points of view the Kashmir experience has been of the highest value in the organization of India's defence.

The partition also created new problems for India in the field of defence. Before August 1947, the frontier of India on the north-west was on the main along a line extending from Gilgit in the Pamirs to the Arabian sea-coast. Broadly speaking it was a natural and defensible frontier. For over a hundred years Britain had carefully studied all the military, political, strategic and other aspects of this area and had worked out an elaborate system for its defence. The Khyber Pass, though historically it had never been the pass of invasion, had become a symbol of British defensive arrangements. The partition of India altered all this. All the prepared areas of defence went to Pakistan.

So far as India was concerned her boundary was marked on the map with no natural defences in respect of Pakistan. The line ran from Kashmir to the Rann of Kutch, which apart from the areas in Kashmir ran through a broad plain that had been divided not on any natural basis but on the basis of the religion of the majority of population occupying the area. Nowhere in the world, except between Canada and U.S.A., is there an international boundary of this nature.

If, as had been vainly hoped, the two new states had started their careers as independent nations with friendly feelings towards each other, the common defence of the subcontinent would have been possible and it would have eliminated much of the trouble. But that was not to be. For reasons which it is not necessary for us to go into here, India and Pakistan settled down to a period of hostility. The struggle in Kashmir was only the most dramatic of the many quarrels which vitiated their relationship. The Indo-Pakistan frontier, both in the west and in the east, had therefore to be considered from the point of view of active defence.

The enormous length of this line, on the western side, extending from the high Karakoram to the Arabian Sea, itself created a formidable problem. Of this length, over a third was through the open plains of the Punjab where armies faced each other. Further south, the line passed mainly through the heart of the great Indian desert. To the north of the Punjab lay the actual line of Kashmir fighting, watched over by an international team for ensuring the observance of truce. The line dividing East Pakistan from India was even more difficult. There the boundary has been for some time subject to alarums and excursions with Pakistan putting forward claims to areas and forcibly occupying them and with India often retaliating.

It is obvious that the creation of two independent states on the subcontinent had itself brought into existence new problems of defence for both countries. But the circumstances following the partition made the problem more acute. Pakistan was created as a " homeland " for Indian Muslims ; but the new state did not include any area which the Muslims of India had traditionally looked upon as centres of their culture and past greatness : Delhi, Agra, Lucknow, or Hyderabad. The self-image of the Indian Muslims had been that of conquerors who coming from outside had established empires in India and ruled the subcontinent for over 600 years. Whatever the truth of this claim, it is undeniable that the general Muslim point of view in regard to India was that it had been a part of the Muslim world and that the Hindus, a race whom they had conquered and ruled, had usurped the inheritance of the Moghuls without any justification. " Khoon se lainge Hindustan . . ." (with blood we shall take Hindustan), became their slogan during the first years of independence. Even before the partition took place Mr. Jinnah and his followers were negotiating with some of the princes to project Pakistan's influence and authority into the new Indian state.

Such projects as the attempt to get Jodhpur to accede to Pakistan, a confederation of princely states stretching from Bhopal to the Arabian Sea (popularly known as the corridor of Kutch), and the annexation of Junagadh on the Kathiawad coast, apart from intrigues in regard to Hyderabad, had clearly shown that in Pakistan's view India would disintegrate and it was for her then to re-establish a Muslim dominion over the whole sub-continent. The failure of the intrigue with the princes and the liquidation of Hyderabad as a centre of Muslim resistance foiled these attempts, but they had the effect of awakening India to a sense of the importance of defence. For the first time new India became frontier-minded.

The inimical attitude of Pakistan showed itself in other ways also. For the first five years after independence Pakistan sought to build up under her leadership a pan-Islamic grouping in the international field, directed mainly against India. Chaudhari Khaliquz-Zaman, the successor of Mr. Jinnah as the President of the Muslim League, even declared in a public statement that the integration of India into a state of 350 million people made it necessary for the Muslims of the Middle East to federate with Pakistan. If such a vision recalled to Muslim minds the glories of Mahmud of Ghazni and the invasions of Mohammed Ghori and the period of Muslim rule in North India, equally in the minds of the people of India it raised the vision of misery and political subordination to which they were not prepared to subject themselves again. In the circumstances, defence arrangements became a major preoccupation of India, not only from the point of view of army organization, but also of laying the foundations of a system of defence based on her own industrial and other potentials.

If the partition of the country, and the events that followed it, made India defence-conscious, events across her Himalayan frontier added new and unforeseen complexities to the problem. In October 1949, two years after India's independence, the Peoples' Republic of China was proclaimed in Peking. This government, for the first time after the early Manchus, was organized in a manner capable of enforcing its authority over the length and breadth of the land.

Organized under communist leadership, it was determined to become in as short a time as possible, a great power in every sense of the word. In 1950, by a combined process of intimidation and negotiation, it brought the vast area of Tibet under its effective authority.

Gradually the Chinese army moved in and by 1956, on the entire boundary from Ladakh to N.-E.F.A. on the Burmese border, the Chinese established their check posts and other agencies of effective border control. That these border forces sometimes clashed and that often there were claims and counter-claims made in respect of certain areas is not the point sought to be emphasized here. The important consideration is that for the first time the Himalayan region became a live frontier after having remained dead all through history.

The boundary between India and China, from the Pamirs to the border of Burma, is in part determined by tradition and usage, partly (in the case of Ladakh) by history, and partly it is demarcated by an agreement between the Tibetan and Indian Governments by what is known as the McMahon line which the Chinese, though they initialled the original document, did not ratify. Though on the Indian side the border was well known, it had never been properly held or its defence arrangements carefully considered or undertaken.

As long as Tibet was ruled by its Dalai Lama, there was no question of the area developing into a major centre of tension. For the first time in history, a great military power stretched out its arm to the Himalayan frontiers and the whole area became transformed into something vital and dynamic. Passes and areas, which no one had heard about, suddenly acquired a new importance. Maps became significant and India realized that she had, as a result of international changes, acquired a new frontier along the Himalayas, the defence of which she had to consider carefully.

The possibility of a new situation developing all along her Himalayan frontiers was realized early by India. She did not wait for the danger to materialize before she began to take necessary precautions. The treaty with Bhutan was re-negotiated and strengthened. In Sikkim, whose defence was solely the responsibility of the Government of India, the civil administration was strengthened and the border areas in Assam were reconstituted into a special administration known as the North East Frontier Agency. The line of India's effective occupation was taken up to the McMahon line. Actually India showed her full awareness of the changed situation in Tibet by steadily developing her defence potential along the Assam frontier, where the lower valleys of Tibet meet India.

The new situation that has developed both as a consequence of independence and as a result of the natural development of events during the period, has changed basically the character of the defence problems of India. Under the British there was never any effective threat from across India's land frontiers. The sea was under the domination of Britain. In the air also the period before the second Great War saw no threat to

India. The range, speed and striking power of the pre-war aeroplanes were such that most air strategists at the time considered India an " air island " not easily vulnerable to air attack.

All this has changed so radically that the defence problem of India today bears no resemblance to the problems that Britain had to face during the hundred and fifty years of her connections with India. As we have seen, the land frontier has become a live one on the western, eastern and northern boundaries. Where there was no major power touching the Indian border which could challenge the armed might of the Anglo-Indian empire, the position is totally different today. Pakistan, armed and trained by the United States, is a considerable power in relation to India, while China though her seat of dynamic power is far away from the Indian border, can bring considerable military strength to bear on any part of the Sino-Indian border.

The situation therefore has undergone a basic change. The defence problems of India are no longer what they were under the British. They have to be thought out and formulated afresh in terms of the altered political and other circumstances of Asia. It is to this task we shall now turn.

CHAPTER IV

THE NEW PROBLEMS

As WE have already noticed defence problems which Britain faced in India were in many ways different from what independent India has to face. India only provided the manpower for the forces which Britain maintained in India. All other factors were supplied by Britain. Essential arms and equipment were supplied by British industry. Even the requirements of transport were based on British supplies.

It was the naval supremacy of Britain which made this divided arrangement for defence possible, for without an absolute and uncontested control of the sea, this system could not have been maintained for any length of time. The failure of sea power at the critical moment led to the surrender of York Town and the loss of America. The temporary loss of control over the Bay of Bengal and the Arabian Sea, following the Japanese conquest of Singapore, left India dangerously exposed for over a period of two years. These two instances should prove how British naval supremacy was during all this period an essential factor in the defence of India. If the army was predominantly Indian, the naval defence till the twenties of this century was the function of the British. The defence of India's shores and of the sea lanes for her communications with England was the responsibility of the Royal Navy.

Moreover Britain never seriously considered her position in India as being directly threatened by a major power. Neither the Russian threat nor the German efforts to outflank sea power could have developed into a serious menace without first disabling Britain in Europe. The reply to all such danger was not on the Indian border but on the battlefields of Europe. Consequently, so far as India's defence was concerned, it was organized to meet the hostilities of untamed tribes on the frontier and to put down any possibility of internal rebellion. The Indian army as we noticed before fulfilled the further function of being a major instrument of imperial policy in the East.

This was a sufficient system of defence as the history of a hundred years demonstrated till Britain's power on the seas was directly challenged by Japan. The Anglo-Japanese hostilities in 1941 exposed the fallacies of Britain's former thinking on Indian defence. With the fall of Singapore the naval supremacy of Britain which was the sure foundation of her defence of India disappeared for a time.

Based as the Indian army's equipment and supplies were on British industries, the arrangements in India for defence against an advancing enemy were found to be utterly inadequate. There was no air strength based in India ; no adequate defence against air attacks. Also the problems of civilian morale behind the lines became a serious matter for the first time, for the conflict threatened to extend to India itself. In these circumstances there was a serious breakdown of India's defence arrangements from the effects of which India was saved by the overwhelming strength which America was able to bring to bear in the Pacific.

When first the Japanese forces occupied Burma, India was caught unprepared ; the British authorities were even prepared to withdraw to Allahabad while in South India the panic was so great that arrangements were made to evacuate Madras and establish the administration in the interior. Fortunately for India the Japanese had to turn back to fight the Americans off the Coral Islands and the threat did not immediately materialize, thereby allowing Britain time to build up her forces in India.

The lesson, however, was salutary. The defence of India could no longer be confined to the manning of frontier posts and vigilance at the Khyber Pass, with an army mainly depending for its armament and munitions on Britain. Also in the changed circumstances, the Indian navy had to become a force sufficiently strong to guard India's coastlines. An independent air force, an industrial base broad enough to equip and maintain the army and finally a national identification with defence, these would have become important factors in India's defence, even if India had not become fully independent. With independence the whole problem required consideration in a different context. India had to shed much of her previous British thinking on the issue and slowly to work out a programme of military defence, taking into consideration the dynamic changes that had taken place all over Asia.

The essential problem of Indian defence as it presented itself to Indian leaders was, how to create a modern defence force of all arms capable of defending India's freedom and of preserving her hard-won unity. The limitations of her position were clear enough. As against the nuclear weapons of the great powers she could not build up an effective defence, the only safety lay in keeping out of the way of such powers. Also it was clear from the beginning that, once both the blocs had nuclear weapons, however much they might be useful as deterrents, their usefulness as weapons of warfare had become limited. Defence in the usual sense was possible only in the case of limited wars with more or less conventional weapons. Also, the lesson that Gandhiji had taught had sunk deep into Indian minds. Superior force can conquer a country, but it cannot keep it down if the weaker nation holds steadfastly to the principles of satyagraha, truth and non-violence.

The case, however, was different in respect of conflicts with conventional weapons. While India might not be able to defend herself against nuclear attack (evidently, no one can) she should be prepared to face any lesser danger and her defence organization must be built up for that purpose. Also it was accepted from the beginning that it should, so far as possible, be based on her own resources. To develop those resources and organize them properly for the purpose of defence was her first responsibility. Has she the resources? Has she the technical skill? Other factors like the sense of national unity, the existence of a stable government and a political structure to which the people as a whole are loyal, the absence of serious social strains, at least to the extent of not affecting national safety, these have to be presumed in the case of nations facing an intense external crisis.

The defence of a country or of a nation's independence is possible only when the people have the determination to defend it, and such determination arises when the factors indicated above exist in a nation. They can be developed and strengthened as a part of an integral defence policy but they must exist independently of the defence forces, if freedom is to be safeguarded and the country effectively defended. We shall discuss these points briefly in a later section.

The problems that the Indian leaders had to face when the question of the reorganization of the defence forces was considered were primarily: had India the resources ? Had she the technical skills ? If she did not have them immediately, could she develop them within a reasonable time ? So far as resources were concerned, it was obvious that India had ample manpower of very high quality, whose bravery, stamina and discipline had been proved on a hundred battlefields. The question whether she had the trained leadership necessary for a modern defence force could not be answered on the basis of experience, as Indian officers did not have the opportunity to command large forces in modern wars. In India itself there was no doubt about it, and considering the level of intelligence and the physical and moral qualities of the officers who had undergone the same training as other officers of the British Indian army, there could be no reasonable doubt about the leadership also. If officers and men were available, the next question was whether there were adequate training facilities in the country.

Unless the troops are trained to the highest pitch, and the officers have an intellectual background and moral discipline which enable them to handle men to the best advantage, every army remains but a mob. It is here that the British had excelled. It is British leadership that had converted the sepoy army into a well-trained force of unexampled prowess. The discipline was excellent and the army as was claimed by the British was made of "tempered steel". India was anxious to maintain and improve the standards which Britain had developed. The new Indian leadership, both political and military, therefore, set itself to do that ; and it may well be said to have improved on the training of the past as it was recognized that the functions of the new army would be somewhat different from those of the British Indian army.

In respect of the training of officers, the problem was more difficult. The British had developed in India only limited facilities for the training of Indian officers, as till the very end the officers of the Indian army had continued to be predominantly British. But even before the withdrawal of the British, this problem had begun to attract attention and without undue delay after independence the existing facilities were expanded to meet most of India's requirements outside the topmost level of training which continued to be in association with Britain. The new academy at Khadakvasla which had been planned as a war memorial is a well-conceived institution modelled on Westpoint, Saint Cyr and other famous colleges of Europe and America.

Apart from training, what is important for an army is to keep in touch with the latest developments in military thinking and to draw from the experience of others. This India has been able to do mainly through her association with Britain and the Commonwealth. A considerable number of the more promising officers are sent every year to Britain to be trained in British institutions in close association with British officers. A certain number go also for staff college and higher training. Since independence India also maintains at her embassies, at all important capitals, military attachés who try to understand the latest developments in military thinking and organization in the countries to which they are accredited. India, in this matter, tries to be up-to-date to the extent of her capacities.

The main problem, apart from the question of training, was the adjustment of the armed forces to the changed political conditions of the country. The army had, at least since the foundation of the Congress (1885), been isolated not only from the national movement but also to a large extent from national sentiment. Everything was done to create a special loyalty not only in the army itself, but in the communities from which the army was recruited.

An elaborate organization was maintained by the army headquarters to look after army pensioners and generally to keep in contact with the recruitment areas and communities and to watch and nip in the bud any growth of nationalist opinion. As the national movement was predominantly Hindu, the British officers in charge of army propaganda developed a special attitude of animosity towards the educated classes among the Hindus — contemptuously referred to as *babus* whose alleged lack of courage and of sturdiness and martial virtues was contrasted unfavourably with the chivalry, sense of loyalty, bravery and other qualities of the martial classes. These ideas, continuously dinned into the ears of the so-called martial classes, succeeded at one time in creating a gulf between the educated classes and the communities which provided the recruits to the army. Their separatism and sense of difference from the rest of the country were encouraged.

The Sikhs, the Rajputs, the Mahrattas, the Garhwalis, the Jats, the Dogras and others among the Hindus from whom a large percentage of the recruits came were made to feel that they were specially favoured communities. The British authorities also encouraged a semi-feudal relationship in the army and the Rajas and Maharajas belonging to these communities were considered and were encouraged to consider themselves their natural leaders.

It was one of the cherished beliefs of the reactionary elements in the British civil and military services that once the controlling hand of Britain was withdrawn, the proud and valiant martial classes, the Rajputs and Sikhs, Jats and others would take no orders from the *pandits* and *banias* in Delhi and would only follow their " natural" leaders : the Jats, the Maharaja of Bharatpur ; the Sikhs, the Maharaja of Patiala, and so on. These prophets of evil were, however, soon disillusioned. The Indian army neither regretted the departure of the British nor showed the least desire to be under their own tribal leaders. In fact, the attempt of one or two of these potentates to claim a special position with the army units recruited from their communities and to be intimately associated with them created resentment among the rank and file of the army.

The Indian army stood like a rock, not merely because of its discipline, but because of the sense of national unity which had grown among its personnel during the interval of the two wars. Also there was the overwhelming sense of crisis arising from the developments on the Indo-Pakistan frontier. The army came out of the crisis as the sword and shield of Indian unity and the danger, if it ever existed outside the fevered imagination of Anglo-Indian Blimps, of the Indian army disintegrating failed altogether to materialize.

The transformation of the army into a truly national force was rendered easy by the necessity forced on India by the withdrawal of British troops to enlarge her own army. It was thus possible to recruit from the excluded classes, without immediately affecting the class composition of the units of the old army.

It may also be emphasized that the difference between the military and non-military classes had reference only to recruitment to the non-commissioned ranks of the army. The new corps of officers which came into existence during the inter-war period and the large-scale recruiting of temporary officers during the war were broadly on a national basis and did not lay emphasis on martial and non-martial classes. Thus, among the more senior officers there was a large percentage from Bengal, Andhra, Madras, Coorg, Kerala and other areas generally neglected from the point of view of army recruitment. The prejudice against the non-martial classes had in fact worn a little thin.

Also, the changed character of war had begun to have an influence on this kind of thinking. Modern warfare required an intelligent, educated army, with specialized skills. Map reading, the handling of wireless, radar and other specialized instruments, mechanical aptitudes, ability to handle complicated machinery : these assumed greater importance than before and became essential for a modern army. This had already become noticeable in the second World War.

The Madrasi regiments, generally not supposed by the Anglo-Indian army chiefs to belong to the martial classes, did extraordinarily well in the field. In the same way, many of the new regiments recruited without reference to the old style of distinctions came out well in training. Consequently, no one was sorry to see the old distinction go. But at the same time it was necessary to prevent any discontent growing in the old recruiting areas as a result of lesser opportunities for a military career, to which the population had been traditionally wedded. This, as we noticed before, was possible as India had to increase her standing army to fill the gap created by the withdrawal of the British units. The new units recruited to take their place wiped out the division which had offended Indian sentiment for a long time and by the same process converted the army from a sectional interest into a national force.

In a country of the size of India with its diverse peoples, each large enough to constitute a state, with its different languages and traditions, the army can either be a laboratory of national union, a strong bond holding together the different sections or can itself become a divisive force.

If the army is, for example, predominantly from one community or area, it could easily give the impression that one area in the country is lording over the others and may therefore be the cause of grave disaffection. Equally, if it represents a narrow ruling class, it might become the instrument of sectional oppression. On the other hand it could also be a unifying factor, bringing together in one central organization elements from every part and giving them the impress of a single nationality.

It could be a major force in the development of national character, because the ex-servicemen, disciplined, educated and with a common national outlook, spread all over the country, could be the nucleus of a new type. The armed forces educate the recruits from different parts of India in a common language, give them a common approach to problems, instil in them the sense of a common nationality and of devotion to the country. Since the service is long term, that is, not a conscript service of two or two and a half years but extending over twenty years, the character of the service is not only stamped on a recruit, but he retires early enough to play a role in the countryside from where he was recruited. The policy of the government being to look after the interest of ex-servicemen, to give them prestige and influence in their areas, the armed forces in service as well as on retirement can become a major factor in the development of India's national unity. This aspect of the building up of India's defence forces will be discussed later.

The creation of a suitable officer cadre, not only efficient and honest, but with a sense of discipline, loyalty and high feeling of patriotism is the steel frame of every modern army. It is on the officer cadre that the army's organization rests. As we have seen, where the Indian military tradition failed before the British period was in not developing an officer corps.

The strength of the British Indian army was not only its training and discipline, but also its leadership, trained, graded, with incentives to take initiative and with a tradition and a code of honour. The higher grades of officers had also knowledge of military problems, had studied military history and were reasonably well informed about military developments elsewhere.

As a foreign corps officering units consisting of people of a different race, and held responsible to lead them in peace and in war the British officers had, broadly speaking, not only a sense of patriotism, but a feeling that if they failed in their duty they would be letting down their own people. They cultivated a spirit of *camaraderie* in their messes, kept themselves sternly aloof from political controversies and took a deep interest in the welfare of their soldiers. The British officer corps of the Indian army built up a great tradition on which, at least in part, rested the greatness of that army.

Could India build up an officer cadre of similar quality and maintain those undoubtedly valuable traditions? It is not merely a question of replacing the British officers, but of maintaining a continuous stream of equal if not superior quality. For this, India has undoubtedly a large reservoir to draw from.

The army of today is popular and can attract to its services the best type of youth. The prestige and social position which belong to the officers are high enough to give the youth an incentive in competing for service as officers. The method of selection ensures quality and eliminates, so far as possible, nepotism and corruption. The officers receive adequate all round training, bringing out both their quality of leadership and their ability to understand the problems of modern warfare, apart from acquiring the special skills required for their particular branches of service. India should therefore find no difficulty in providing her armed forces with a continued supply of officers of high quality.

What then is the problem? The problem is to keep the officer cadre contented. The Indian army is organized on the basis of long-term service. Officering is a career in itself, honourable, well-paid and with a few glittering prizes at the end. But the conditions of service in the armed forces require that officers retire at an age when in civil employment they are only half way through their career. The vast majority of officers retire when they have reached their colonelcy or equivalent rank in other service. Not even if an officer reaches one of the coveted positions, as corps commander or principal staff officer, could he stay in active service as long as the civilian officer.

Briefly it means that at a comparatively early age when in other spheres of life a man is considered as reaching the period of his best work, and is beginning to earn a comfortable salary, the army officer is retired from service with an inadequate pension. This period of life is particularly important.

At the age of forty-five a man's children are still at school; at least another ten or twelve years of heavy responsibility and expenditure for the education of children and the marriage of his daughters lie before him. His pension as a colonel would hardly enable him to live in comfort. He will undoubtedly have to find employment which would bring him a reasonable salary. But except in the case of army engineers and medical men, the normal officers are not trained for ordinary civil careers requiring specialized skills. All their training is in the leadership of men and their claim for civil appointments is based on an aptitude for *bandobast* or executive ability. How is an officer at the age of forty-five or fifty to adjust himself in the competitive world.

This is the problem which worries the young officer and which should worry every government. In former times the matter was not of such grave consequence. The army officers in England, for example, normally came from well-to-do families and to them the pension on retirement was an addition to the normal income.

So long as the officer classes were recruited from a prosperous middle class, social rank and glamour were sufficient incentives. But economic conditions in India today do not allow for the growth of a well-to-do middle class, with the consequence that the financial aspect of an officer's career has become particularly important at the present time. Unless the conditions of service are satisfactory, and the officers on retirement are assured of absorption into industry or other government services giving an adequate return, the new officer class will become increasingly disgruntled, thereby affecting the efficiency of our armed forces.

Again, there are such problems as the provision of facilities for education for officers' children. By the nature of their service all but a few of the officers of the armed forces will be serving away from cities, in cantonments and in special centres where it is impossible to provide facilities for higher education. This is not merely a question affecting officers but all defence force personnel.

The British Government in India gave careful attention to this problem, as it affected the children of soldiers and non-commissioned officers and established special schools for them. The problem of the education of officers' children did not arise during the British period as there were but few Indian officers. But, today this forms an important aspect of the nation's treatment of the military personnel and a policy which while not separating them from the general community will remove the handicaps from which their children now suffer would appear to be necessary.

In every civilized modern community, the subordination of the military to the civil authority is an accepted principle ; it is an essential and overriding doctrine in all democracies. It follows as a result, not only that the army should be subordinate to civil authorities, but that the primacy of the civil government should be emphasized at all times. The officers of the army can nowhere claim privileges which their *confréres* in civil government do not enjoy. This being granted, it is equally necessary to emphasize that unless the officer cadres feel that their interests are safe in the hands of the civil authority, and that there is no great disparity between civil and military personnel of similar rank and service, and that in such matter as in employment, after their period of service they will have the active support of civil authorities, the whole morale of the army as an instrument of civil government may be undermined. It should never be forgotten that without the officer cadre the army is but a collection of men — a mob.

For the reasons indicated earlier, the defence of India's sea coasts was never a problem for the British. From the time of the great French Admiral Sufferen's departure from the Indian seas in 1784 till the fall of Singapore during the second World War, the Indian Ocean was a British lake and no threat of any kind could possibly have arisen to the security of India from the sea side. True, the growth of Japan's naval power in the Pacific changed the nature of the problem from what it was in the nineteenth century; and after the Washington Conference of 1923 Britain awoke to the necessity for regional navies not so much as independent units, but to get round the ratio of 5 : 5 : 3 which had been laid down under the treaty.

Japan's strength was in her own and in Chinese waters : there she no doubt had the advantage over other powers, whose responsibilities were world wide; but that she would be able to threaten British supremacy in the Bay of Bengal was not thought of even as a possibility. Therefore, though the Indian navy came to have a separate existence from 1924 it was only as a minor wing of the British grand fleet, and not even as a task force capable of defending its own regional waters.

The second World War showed how fallacious were the assumptions of India's naval defence. Once the Singapore bastion was breached the Mikado's ships roamed the Indian seas unchallenged by the Royal Navy which was tied with the defence of Britain's own lifelines. It was the timely intervention of the American navy in the South Pacific that saved India from the threat that the Japanese control of the Bay of Bengal posed to her defence. Slowly by the end of the war the Japanese navy had been swept out of the Indian Ocean. But the danger that the incident disclosed was something which could not easily be forgotten. India's naval defence was of primary importance and could no longer be neglected.

But the problem was not an easy one. India's own naval traditions, though highly significant in the earlier periods of her history, were only local. The great Indian empires based on the North Indian plains never developed any effective naval tradition, and as we have emphasized, Britain did not find it necessary to develop an Indian navy as the Royal Navy was always available for the defence of every part of the empire. A new tradition had to be created. During the British period Indian navy could still be considered a subordinate arm. But with independence the whole position changed. The navy had to be developed as a self-contained unit capable of effectively contributing to the defence of India and of maintaining in times of peace India's authority in the waters around her.

During the war the Indian navy served with the highest distinction, not only in the Arabian Sea and the Indian Ocean, but in association with the Royal Navy in the Mediterranean and the Atlantic. The experience of this working along with the British navy was itself of great importance. Also seeing service in the actual conditions of war in different seas and climes was something which could not fail to fire the imagination of India's seamen. The record of the Indian navy during the war proved conclusively that the spirit of Kanhoji Angre and Kunjali Marakkars was still alive among the peoples of India.

With independence the problem became more acute. The Royal Indian Navy, as a part of the imperial forces, could be a supplementary arm, a subordinate regional unit and not a self-contained force. But the navy of independent India, however closely it was to be associated with the British navy, could not be a subordinate branch, dependent on the naval staff and higher command of Britain. It had to develop as an independent force, with every branch necessary for a modern navy, shore installations, repair bases, training schools for general staff — apart of course from a balanced force of all types of units, cruisers, destroyers, frigates, minesweepers, aircraft carriers, submarines and torpedo boats, and an adequate naval air arm, etc.

Obviously, it was impossible to create a whole navy all at once. It had to be built up slowly; India did not possess the industrial potential to build her own naval units. They had, therefore, to be acquired from others, Britain in this case. Not only had the ships to be acquired but the ratings and officers had to be trained for the special kind of work each of these units required. It had to be a slow and painful process, as naval ships are among the most costly things in the world, both to acquire and to keep up. But India having become independent had to face the responsibilities of independence.

CHAPTER V

THE NEW PATTERNS OF DEFENCE

IN THE nuclear age there is, it would appear, no adequate measure of defence against the total destructiveness of the new weapons, guided missiles, hydrogen bombs and similar instruments of annihilation. The only method of escape is to anticipate the enemy and destroy him, or keep out of his way. By avoiding him, it is possible to resist him through non-violence, satyagraha and other tried methods of the physically weak. There is, however, one fairly sure method of escape from nuclear destruction, and that is the possession of similar weapons by more than one state.

The disappearance of monopoly in nuclear weapons is undoubtedly an effective deterrent, for rivalry and competition in this dangerous sphere may be said to nullify the offensive possibilities of nuclear warfare. In any case, so far as India is concerned, she does not desire to arm herself with nuclear weapons nor is her defence organized to meet attacks from powers armed to destroy not only their enemies but humanity itself.

Even among the great powers, armed with nuclear weapons, it is not clear that in the future these states will resort to nuclear warfare except in cases of extreme danger. Moreover, in India's case it is clear that her defence has to be in terms of her geographical situation, leaving the possibility of nuclear attack by a great power out of consideration. An attack that she has to envisage can only be with conventional weapons along her frontiers by land and sea and air. Her defence is therefore basically the defence of the frontiers, organized in such a manner that the civilian life inside the country is not disrupted or even seriously affected.

Such a war, though limited in the sense that only certain types of weapons will be used, will in other respects be a total war, that is, it will be a war not merely between the organized armed forces of the countries, but between the peoples themselves. Till 1914 wars were conducted between armies and victory or defeat was determined by the comparative strength of the armed forces and the skill with which they were led. But the war of 1914 and to a greater extent the second World War disclosed the new features of the total war.

War, of course, continued as before to be a conflict between armed forces, but its nature was extended. Civil life behind the army lines came under heavy attack. The industrial and economic life of the enemy country, its railways and communication system, its ports and harbours and all other centres of its active life came under attack. The objective was not merely to defeat the army in the battlefield but to disrupt its communications, render difficult the production of essential commodities, not only arms and other military supplies, but even food for civilians at home, reduce the enemy's morale and break his will to fight. Nothing was considered sacred or beyond the scope of attack.

In the first Great War, a few shells on the Cathedral of Rhiems shocked the moral opinion of the world. But in the Second War the damage to sacred edifices was so extensive that neither party complained, or made much of it. The bombardment of Guernica in the Spanish Civil War was considered a major act of inhumanity; but Coventry in England and almost all the major towns in Germany suffered so much damage that the destruction of Guernica paled into insignificance before such large-scale acts of inhumanity. The fact is that the frontline and the inner lines of war have got inextricably mixed up and warfare today is between nations and not merely between armed forces on land, sea and air.

If the character of warfare has changed fundamentally in this manner, it is obvious that the pattern of defence cannot have remained static. Defence has to be not merely by the armed forces but by the whole nation. Total defence was first preached by Barres during the French Revolution, for the accepted rule even in his time was for offensive war to be confined to the armed forces and for the civilian population to be left, broadly speaking, unmolested. Such an attitude had not been strictly accepted in civil wars, which were at all times more bitter than other forms of conflict and fought with little reference to the conventions of civilization. But in the wars between nations, among civilized people, warfare till the end of the nineteenth century was confined to fights between trained forces of warfare.

In India from the earliest times, the general population, except in case of national revolts, was unconcerned with fights between armies. Especially in the eighteenth century, in the struggle for empire which, when it ended in 1818, gained for Britain the empire of India, the wars left the population unmoved, though their sufferings were great. This was perhaps due to the fact that in the Carnatic and in Bengal national sentiment was not engaged and the fight was between a trading company and pretenders to office who had no claim to the loyalty of the people. Whatever the reasons, except in the campaigns against the Mahrattas and against the Sikhs, the British authorities never had to fight forces which were backed by a sense of nationhood.

During the British period, as we noticed, a gulf was created between the army and the civilian public so that it would have been surprising if there was any active sympathy between the two. But it had never in fact to be put to test for the battles which the British and Indian armies had to fight after 1858 were fought outside the territories of India.

The problem today is different. If India has on her two land frontiers powerful neighbours she has also a burning sense of nationality and a determination to defend her freedom at all costs. The pattern of Indian defence has, therefore, to be different from what it was in the past. This pattern, it is obvious, has to be based on the total effort of the nation in all essential fronts, in the defence forces, in the industrial and agricultural fields, in civilian morale, in the capacity to maintain essential activities under the most trying circumstances, and in continued research in sciences and in all matters relating to national survival. A defence system which does not take into consideration all these facts cannot survive in modern wars.

In essence, therefore, it is not merely a question of the defence forces, though at all times they have to form the iron ring inside which other national activities can go on undisturbed. If the armed forces fail or are destroyed or scattered in battles all other factors of defence are rendered practically helpless. It is, however, equally true that with the best army in the world, equipped with the best weapons, no country can win a war if the civilian morale breaks down and the homefront cracks up. Without industrial and armament production keeping up with requirements, without an adequate supply of food, with widespread social unrest behind the fighting lines, no country can win a war. The defence organization, therefore, is not merely the organization of the different arms of fighting forces, but the coordination of national effort in every sphere.

The most important factor in national defence has to be the quality of the forces. This includes training, morale, equipment, leadership and all other factors which make the fighting forces efficient. The evolution of warfare from the earliest days has depended on the organization and training of the fighting forces. Unfortunately, Indian tradition of warfare was not based on any scientific theory of training. It was based on the use of masses of men, with the backing of trained elephants and with warriors fighting in chariots.

The use of units of infantry trained to fight in closed formation giving support to each other and fighting as one arm which multiplied the strength of individuals was one of the most revolutionary discoveries in history. That such close knit and disciplined units fighting under trained leadership can defeat vastly superior numbers in battle has been proved in a hundred fields. The Greek phalanx, the Roman legions and other infantry formations changed the nature of warfare. This system never seems to have effectively reached India before the eighteenth century.

An equally revolutionary transformation in the method of warfare was the use of cavalry. In India, as in all other countries in the earlier periods, horses were used in war for drawing chariots. It is the Central Asian nomads who made it an irresistible arm of fighting, by training the horse in such a manner as to enable a horseman riding on it to charge at the enemy and sabre him. The invention of the stirrup by which it became possible for a horseman to discharge arrows while riding made the cavalry the most irresistible force before machine-guns and tanks came into use.

The Hindus, however, did not take kindly to the use of cavalry. Till the twelfth century, cavalry does not seem to have been widely used in Indian fighting and the trained elephant though difficult to manoeuvre and lacking in speed, was able to hold its own on the battlefield. But with the arrival of the cavalry with Mohammed Ghori the elephant became a handicap.

All through this period of Indian history from the invasion of Mohammed and Kutub-ud-Din Aibak to the time of the rise of the Mahratta power, the Muslim rulers were invariably described in Sanskrit works as *Aswapatis* or lords of horses while the Hindu rulers were known as *Gaiapatis* or lords of elephants. Similar was the position in regard to cannon. The Indian rulers never really took to artillery. The casting of cannon under the Moghuls was entrusted to foreigners while the artillery was manned mainly by Rumis or Turks. The Mahratta artillery at Panipat was under Ibrahim Gardi. The failure of Indian rulers to withstand British attack was essentially a failure to master technology and their inability to cast and use artillery.

This historic weakness we have overcome as a result of our British tutelage. The sepoy army of the British was superbly trained. Its discipline was perfect. It was also efficiently led by British officers. The result was that in every battlefield in Europe, Africa and Asia it was able to stand up against the best trained armies, against the Germans in France, Africa and Italy and against the Japanese in Burma. Independent India has taken the fullest care to see that these three factors, training, discipline and leadership, are fully maintained and strengthened in the new Indian army.

So far as training is concerned, not only has India created new training institutions of every kind for her army but has also, so far as possible, kept the training up-to-date, incorporating features from the experience of other great nations. Apart from special institutions for giving specialized training and experience, like the artillery school and mountain warfare school, the main centres of basic training are at Khadakvasla, near Poona, and at Dehra Dun. A new defence college for senior officers is also being established in Delhi.

The Khadakvasla institution, though planned during the last days of British authority as a war memorial, was brought into existence by the independent Government of India, incorporating many new features, which the experience of the war and the changed conditions in India rendered advisable. It is, in its broad outline, a kind of military university where cadets are admitted at the age of fifteen, and given a general course of education under strict military discipline before they are trained to be officers of the various arms of the defence force, army, navy or air force. A higher standard of general education is insisted upon, before specialized training begins. The cadets, before they choose their separate careers, are brought up together ensuring a sense of fellowship among the officers of the three arms of the service. Also for developing national sentiment in the forces the significance of having young men from different parts of India living under the same roof and under the same discipline and undergoing the same training could not be overestimated.

After the preliminary training at Khadakvasla the cadets of the different services go to their own institutions which are maintained in different parts of India. The training, of course, does not cease with the award of commissions. It is as elsewhere a continuous process at specialized institutions.

Nor has higher training been neglected. The Staff College at Wellington not only maintains the traditions of the original college at Quetta but has developed along new lines. The new National Defence College at Delhi is meant for higher training of senior officers of the three services.

In respect of the navy and the air force also the Government of India have been farsighted enough to establish essential training centres. So far as the navy is concerned, these training institutions follow the British model, and arrangements exist for the higher training of Indian naval personnel with British establishments on board the British vessels. The superior training in the air force is not solely British. As a proportion of the fighters was acquired from France, the training in respect to them has to be in France. The Government of India is following a determined policy of providing adequate training institutions at all levels. This is indeed vital, for the best equipment is nothing without trained personnel behind it. The more complicated and more effective the machine is, the higher the degree of intelligence and training required to manage it. Also its production requires a very high degree of training and skill. The dependence on trained and disciplined personnel has become greater and not less with the modernization of the armed forces.

The main weakness of India's defence lies in the fact that for the heavier arms and equipment she is still dependent on foreign supply. In respect of the weapons of the army, India does not produce many items of high importance in her weaponry. She is, for the time being, dependent on foreign supply for tanks, armour-piercing guns and other heavier weapons and equipment. Even for mechanized transport the army has so far had to depend mainly on imported trucks and weapon-carriers and other vehicles. In these matters, however, effective steps have been taken to remedy the position.

Arrangements are being made for the gradual manufacture of all essential requirements in India itself, directly under the control of the Defence Department where private industry is unable immediately to take the work in hand. This has to be a phased programme spread over years, but even then it is not to be expected that India could be completely independent of foreign supply in respect of many complicated items till she has reached a much higher state of industrialization. Under the present policy where the production is useful both for defence and for general purposes, as in the case of electronics, on which defence depends for radars and other highly specialized devices and the civil population for radio and other supplies, Government has taken the initiative in establishing public corporations for the creation and development of the industry. But the weakness still remains though with the increasing industrialization the present dependence on foreign supplies will diminish rapidly and disappear in time.

So far as the air force and the navy are concerned though India has started on a modest scheme of production, it is obvious that for at least a considerable time to come she will not be able wholly to depend upon herself for the construction of different types of aircraft and the more complex types of naval vessels. No doubt, either under licence or in cooperation with outside firms, India will soon produce aeroplanes in her own factories. That, though important, is not the entire problem.

The essential thing in air defence is that production of aircraft should keep pace with the latest improvements which advanced research introduces into the production of other countries. It is not sufficient that India produces for her own use bombers and other aircraft. If Indian production under licence is based on types already in existence, they would almost certainly have been outmoded by other types, by the time India begins to produce them. This is inevitable and the experience in the last war should prove to us that the basic strength of a country's armed forces depends upon the superiority of the arms they use.

The experience of Japan should provide us with an effective warning in this matter. Neither in patriotism, nor in courage, nor again in discipline, determination and readiness for sacrifice were the Japanese in any way inferior to their enemies. But they were definitely inferior in one vital respect. They could not keep pace with American production or with the improvements introduced by American research in aircraft and naval construction. So the defeat of Japan was due to her inferiority in scientific research and that is a lesson no one can afford to forget.

CHAPTER VI

DEFENCE AND CIVIL SOCIETY

As WE have tried to emphasize, warfare today is not confined to encounters between armies and other trained forces. It extends to all dimensions.

As warfare is total, defence has also to be total. During the second World War this became an axiom. Not only had industrial labour producing munitions and other essential things for the conduct of war been considered as part of national service, but farmwork for the production of food, transport workers, without whom the produce of industry could not be removed to the warfront, home guards, fire fighters and numerous other similar organizations meant to ensure civilian life and protect it from enemy action became important aspects of defence. In fact, with the development of air warfare and V 2 weapons, not only the fighting line but also the total area of the community at war became a warfront. The problems of defence in this area are different from what they are in the frontline.

A country whose morale has been weakened by enemy propaganda or through its own internal contradictions, falls an easy prey to the enemy, even as the body whose resistance has been weakened falls a prey to disease. National discipline is therefore an essential aspect of today's defence. Traditionally India had never subscribed to this point of view, as with the exception of the Mahrattas, the general point of view of Indian states in the past had been that warfare was the business of the fighting forces and it was the business of the civilian population to accept the result without murmur. Such an attitude arose out of the old theory of warfare that civil life should not, as far as possible, be disturbed as a result of war.

The great modern wars fought by Britain on India's borders were not national wars and the civil population did not feel themselves committed one way or the other or consider their interests as being irrevocably involved. The general attitude in India during the two Great Wars was unfriendly to Britain and while not desiring her total defeat, welcomed a weakening of her power. The efforts which Britain in the later years of the second World War made to consolidate national opinion by such organizations as the National War Front and by radio and other forms of publicity had but little effect on the Indian public. This was not because the Indian people were not patriotic but because they could not identify their patriotism with British authority in India.

In the circumstances of today the situation would not be the same but it must be recognized that with our inadequate national integration, the danger of civilian morale breaking down behind the frontline could not be overlooked. Even in well-integrated countries, like France during the last war, the first serious impact of defeat led to a demoralization which came as a surprise to the world. In India which for a century has been unaccustomed to war, the effect of half a dozen bombs falling in a major city like Bombay, Delhi or Calcutta may be utter chaos, while a serious and concentrated attack on centres of industry or on vital points of communications may bring to the surface many ugly features of our national life leading to a breakdown of transport and the prevalence of anarchy over large areas. As any war in the future, however limited, would necessarily involve bombing of the interior lines, strategic places and major centres of production — apart also from horror bombing in " soft " areas — this aspect of strengthening the civil population should be considered one of the essential parts of any defence system.

How is this to be achieved in a country with four hundred million people whose integration is still imperfect and whose population which though prepared to suffer calamities of fate stoically, had not during a hundred years been subjected to strains and stresses resulting from warfare? The only effective method is to create a sense of national discipline by organized effort. This is not an easy task but can be done by a determined and consistent policy carried on over a period.

It is universally recognized that human beings organized in groups shed their fear more easily and act with courage which individually they do not feel. The whole theory of disciplined group action in war is based on this principle. Thus while individuals feel panicky in certain situations, company gives them courage and determination.

The organization into units of manageable size and building up whole formations on them have been the fundamental development in warfare which as a consequence changed from combats between champions or hurly burly between masses into tactical movements meant to overcome the enemy or to withstand his onslaught. This principle is equally applicable to civilian population.

A sense of national discipline can be infused into the people by organizing them in times of crisis into groups with special functions under trained leadership. Home guards, fire watching units, volunteer companies for social services, these and other forms of organization bringing people together and charging them with collective responsibility were widely used during the last war both to uphold civilian morale and to help in war work. These are generally organized during the time of war but skeleton programmes exist in peacetime together with a trained leadership which can take charge of such programmes when the time comes; otherwise it may be too late.

The danger of a civilian breakdown is mainly in areas of great concentration of people: cities, industrial areas and harbours. It should not be difficult in these places to create and perfect an organization for maintaining civilian morale and discipline in wartime. It is, however, to be remembered that it is the urban population, a large percentage of which have no local roots, that is inclined to panic in times of crisis. The peasant keeps to his little bit of land and in any case, the danger is less in rural areas. The experience of Calcutta where a few Japanese bombs fell should teach us that when it comes to facing a danger of that kind the civilian population in cities will be inclined to run for cover to outlying areas. It is not by making such flights from cities impossible but only by creating organizations to uphold the courage of people that civilian morale could be maintained during a crisis.

How is this to be done? The most satisfactory approach to this problem is to create among the young a sense of hardihood, courage and belief in joint action, qualities which intensive training like scouting could impart to the young. The training of youth in collective organizations would provide not only the necessary leadership in times of crisis, but allow the sense of national solidarity to permeate all classes. Scouting and its equivalent for girls should be made compulsory for all children and it should be pursued with a certain amount of seriousness which would instil in the youth both discipline and the sense of service to the community. At the higher level of the university, this training should be continued in the form of national cadet corps through which a sense of military discipline may reach the higher and educated classes. The maintenance of territorial units and volunteer organizations are also of great value.

No less important for the purpose of building up civilian discipline is the utilization of retired army men. In a country like India, trained servicemen carry in the countryside a prestige and authority which are inestimable assets for the nation. If this prestige is carefully built up and civilian discipline in rural areas is organized around retired officers and men of the armed forces they would provide a steel frame which could be of great use, especially in times of crisis.

Formerly, as the army was recruited only from certain sections classified as martial classes, and some areas like South India and Bengal were excluded from the army, this class of retired army men did not provide a nation-wide basis for action. Also, their loyalty to the British Government made them suspect with the people and this stood in the way of their being considered the natural leaders of the rural community. Today the position is gradually changing. The army is now recruited from all parts of India without reference to caste or community. Also, the armed forces today are national and are recognized and honoured as such. Besides, the old feudal structure having disappeared the retired army personnel have much greater chance today of effectively assuming leadership than at any other time.

These provide the nucleus for an organization to inculcate a sense of national discipline. But beyond all this, there must be the sense of belonging to a community, the conception of a motherland, which is worthy of every sacrifice, a sound integration which makes each group feel itself a part of a wider whole. In India, broadly speaking, these factors had not been conspicuously present in many parts in the past and the basic weakness of her defence could at all times be traced to this.

When the Muslims under Mohammed Ghori invaded the country the powers that fought them had no idea of defending India but only of defending their own kingdoms. Thus the Chauhan monarch who fought Ghori fought for the maintenance of his own power and was not supported by other rulers, and when he failed, the other rulers of North India fell one by one to the invaders. Only when the Muslim invaders reached South India, the feeling was sufficiently aroused among the people as a whole to enable the leaders to organize a movement of national resistance.

The Vijayanagar empire was organized with this declared object in view. It was to safeguard *swadharma* and to uphold *swarajya* that the country south of the Tungabhadra was organized as a single state, after the many principalities into which the area was divided had been swept away by Malik Kaffur. This basic fact that the empire was constituted for the defence of *swadharma* was not for a moment forgotten by the Vijayanagar emperors, as their inscriptions and records testify.

In the Madan Gopalswamy temple inscription, the capital of Vijayanagar is described as Hampi-Hastinavati, thus seeking to identify the empire with the epic tradition of the past and looking upon the rest of India as *terra-irredenta*, temporarily occupied by enemies. A similar tradition develops in North India under

Rajput monarchs, especially Kumba, Sanga and Pratap, who organized national resistance for upholding *swadharma*, as the titles of the *Hindwan Suraj* and *Hindupati* which their successors proudly wore, bear ample witness. Finally the rise of the Mahrattas under Shivaji and his immediate successors had an equally national basis. Even so late as 1801 Arthur Wellesley, later the Duke of Wellington, noted shrewdly that only the Mahrattas of all people in India at the time possessed a sense of nationality.

Apart from these notable instances, the general tendency after the establishment of Muslim power in North India was to identify the state with the dynasty or the community in power, with a consequent absence of any sense of loyalty among the people as a whole. The Muslim dynasties of North India, before the Moghul emperors, were too short-lived, too much given to internecine fights and too fanatical in their attitude towards the Hindu population for a sense of integral nationality to be re-born after the conquest.

After the middle of the fourteenth century, Hindu sentiment had revived even in North India and the dominating political fact was the fight between the two communities. When the Moghuls invaded India the main opposition, it is significant to note, came from the Rajput confederacy under Rana Sanga. The century following the accession of Akbar created for the first time after Mohammed Ghori's invasions the sense of a single political community in India organized as an empire, and for another hundred years the idea of a nation-state, which Akbar created, continued to have its fascination for the Indian mind. The Mahratta sovereign recognized in theory the emperor of Delhi as did the monarchs of the southern extremity of India.

But it was only a vague idea. The effective power of the empire had vanished. Thus after the middle of the eighteenth century, following the intervention in Arcot when the forces of the East India Company came up against the provincial authorities of the empire, the sense of nationality had disappeared and the people of the area, whether of Madras or of Bengal, felt no identification with the Moghul warlords who were trying to convert their offices into hereditary principalities.

The absence of a national feeling in India in the eighteenth century except in the areas under the direct Mahratta administration is a glaring fact. It is with armies raised locally that the Company conquered India. Though the sepoy army felt no territorial loyalty to India they had at different times shown that when it came to their *dharma* they had a loyalty which it was dangerous for their employers to overlook.

The Great Rebellion of 1857-58 convinced the British of this fact. But the upheaval in the sepoy army, it should be noted, was not solely for upholding their *dharma* which they thought was being attacked and undermined, but also had for the first time a political background in terms of India as a single country. The question is not whether that appeal was heeded by all. Obviously, in South India, in the Punjab and in Bengal, the movement hardly found any sympathisers. There is no doubt, however, that the movement, as it developed, had an all-India objective and had the germs of an all-India national sentiment.

Today no one can deny that the sense of nationhood, of belonging to a country of four hundred million people, exerting themselves to be recognized as a progressive community in the world, is the governing fact in Indian life. It pervades all aspects of Indian activity. The pride is undoubtedly that of belonging to a community to which every kind of sacrifice is due. It is more than the old desire to maintain *swadharma*, one's own way of life, though it is an essential part of it. It is basically the desire to remain free, not again to lose the precious heritage that the nation has won after so much struggle and sacrifice, that binds the community together and gives it strength. This is the new vision of India that unites her diverse peoples and gives them an ideal to defend.

Without a vision of one's country, as something worthy of being defended at all costs, national morale will never stand any great strain. At all times of India's past greatness this vision of India existed.

India, the holy land (*punya bhoomi*) extending from the Himalayas to Cape Comorin, was a vision which the people of the Mauryan age undoubtedly had. The *Chakravarti patha* or the territory of the empire is thus described in Kautilya's *Arthashastra*. The author of the *Vishnu Purana* speaks of gods being jealous of the sons of the land of Bharata. All the great rivers of India from the Ganges to Cauvery are held sacred by the Hindus. The places of Hindu pilgrimage are spread all over the country. In fact, the Hindus of ancient times seem to have taken every care to generate and keep alive a sense of India's unity and her sacredness.

But many circumstances contributed to this vision fading at different times. The very size of the country stood in the way of a complete integration. Some of its geographical factors such as the absence of rivers flowing from north to south, the existence of a Deccan massif which gave to the plateau its special features, the peninsular character of the south — these factors in the past had operated against a complete integration of India's peoples. These have been finally overcome, and the vision of the ancient *rishis* of Bharat as a single country has been revived and fully realized now.

In the nineteenth century, the conception of India as one, became a major belief in the Indian mind. Bankim Chandra Chatterji in his famous song *Vande Mataram* gave inspired expression to it. Even Iqbal, the Muslim poet, who later became the advocate of Pakistan, was inspired by this vision of a new and united India and sang of *Hindustan Hamara*. But it was Tagore, the poet of Indian nationhood, who had the complete vision of the motherland and sang of her glory.

This conception of India as one motherland, though inherited by us over a period of two thousand years, has taken a new significance today. We are united in a democratic structure where each part of the country has an equal and honoured place. The Government of India is by the representatives of the entire population of the country, without reference to caste, community or religion. And each part is self-governing so that there can be no sense of grievance, or a feeling that one part of the country is having a predominance over others.

For the first time India is united not merely by a sense of the unity of her culture and civilization, but of the rights and privileges of her people, by the common effort towards her greatness, by the interdependence of her different areas for their own economic welfare and for the prosperity of the whole. Today's vision of India sings of her rivers not as sacred places of pilgrimage, but as the sources of vast irrigation works which provide for the entire country, as suppliers of energy through the giant hydro-electric schemes coming up all over India — in fact it is a new sacredness that the rivers have achieved.

New centres of pilgrimage, created by the mind and vision of man, where one can witness the magical transformation of nature's gifts for the benefit of man — steel towns, factories of all kinds, shipbuilding yards, in fact vast networks of creative activity spread all over India in the building up of which men from every part of India have a share, are arising in different parts of India.

Nor is this all. The benefit of this new activity is to be shared by all. The new India of today provides for all alike. She is the mother not only of the rich and the powerful, of the higher castes and the nobles, but of all alike. It is an egalitarian society that India today represents, where the Brahmin and the Pariah have the same rights, where a conscious effort is being made to eliminate the oppression by one group of another and where no part of the country or no group of people is made to feel that it is inferior to others. Every one, therefore, has an equal interest in the defence of the country.

The essential fact is that without a deep sense of loyalty to the country, felt by the people at large, no effective defence has been possible at any time. In the past this sense of loyalty was generally towards a monarch who symbolized the nation or who represented the *dharma* or the community as the case may be. You fought for the king and in fighting for the king defended the country. As most countries in Europe and in Asia evolved as nations around some dynasty, this loyalty could be equated with loyalty to the state which it legitimately represented. But in the changed circumstances of today, the loyalty to the monarch provides no adequate substitute to a more intense and comprehensive loyalty to the nation.

In India this loyalty to the monarch was a significant fact in early periods. But with the breakdown of the imperial idea in the seventh century A.D. the loyalty to the monarch altogether eclipsed the idea of loyalty to India. The country was split up into many states and none of them had the right to claim the sovereignty of India as a whole. Patriotism therefore became in the period after Harsha, a feeling of regionalism, of allegiance to the local monarch. Thus when the Muslims under Mohammed Ghori invaded India sense of loyalty to India as such had vanished, as the conception of a single India had itself been under eclipse for centuries. It did not however take a long time for a spirit of resistance to the invader to grow. When the North Indian states fell one by one to the onslaught of the Turks and the Afghans, a popular movement began to take the place of political resistance. But that resistance was not based on a sense of loyalty to the country, but to *swadharma*. It was an ideological and not a territorial feeling.

A territorial feeling of nationalism as covering the whole of India, a combination of the feeling of *swadharma* and patriotism began to grow only in the nineteenth century after the Mutiny when the whole of India had come effectively under British rule. This would be clear from the fact that all previous wars and revolts had only a local basis and when such wars could be said to have been for a cause, they were solely for the maintenance of local traditions or regional sovereignties. The Great Rebellion itself visualized India in terms of a decrepit Moghul empire with the emperor reigning in Delhi, but with every local ruler from the *peshwa* in Poona to the *subedar* of little Jhansi exercising his sovereign rights. It is from the ashes of the Rebellion of 1857 that India's nationalism was born. The new nationalism that developed with the Congress was both territorial and ideological. It embodied in its vision the whole of

India and all the races and communities inhabiting it. It also thought in terms of India's own way of life, no doubt reformed and renovated, but having firm roots in India's own traditions.

For the first time after centuries, a new vision of India has come to Indian mind, clear and unmistakable and embodying the hopes and faith of all her people ; something to cherish and to defend ; something before whose security and safety, the voice of controversy is stilled. It is this vision that gives strength to India's defence for where such a vision does not exist, defence becomes a mechanical process. That this is no overstatement may be seen from the fact that even communist Russia, when faced with Hitler's invasion, had, forgetting all communist theories, to exploit the sense of patriotism, and the second World War, so far as Russia is concerned, is still known as the Great Patriotic War. It is when this vision has become faint or has completely faded away that a nation abandons its defence. De Gaulle evoking from London the memory of Joan d'Arc, Churchill from his embattled island summoning the moral opinion of the world to help — these are other recent instances which prove that a clear vision of the community alone gives strength to the defence of a people. This is what India is developing for the first time in recent centuries.

CHAPTER VII

INDUSTRIAL AND PRODUCTIVE STRENGTH IN RELATION TO INDIAN DEFENCE

FROM THE earliest times in man's history two factors, apart from the will to defend, have been decisive in warfare: first, the ability to produce the most effective weapons, and secondly, a safe supply of ample food. When primitive tribes fought against each other, the tribe which had a ready supply of better bows and arrows and which had control of its own fishing and hunting areas, and could not therefore be starved into submission, came out victorious. When man emerged from tribal society and kings fought with regular armies under their command, the situation did not change basically. The side which had the better arms, or better movement and transport, and was better able to use arms and animals through training, discipline and organization, and whose food supply was safe, won over its enemies. When cavalry became the major arm, the rearing of horses became important and the nation which had better horses had an advantage over others. The Roman defeat at Hadrianople in A.D. 378 marked the end of the Legion and established the growing importance of the mounted soldier. The long bow won at Crecy. Artillery again changed the course of warfare. Gustavus Adolphus, by replacing bowmen with musketeers and by introducing field guns and hand grenades, effected a change in the nature of war which has had its influence for centuries. Roon's new gun won at Sedan. In this way every important revolution in warfare was the result either of a new method of organization, the Greek hoplite, the Roman legion or the discovery or use of a new weapon. As weapons were simple in earlier days, the question of industrial organization was not a serious one. And yet the fact that the best armour, the damascene swords and shields, required special skills and were manufactured by certain countries gave them an advantage over others. But actually, till the introduction of cannon in warfare, the question of the productive capacity of a nation did not become the decisive factor in defence. Cannon was not easy to cast. Once cast, its use also required technical skill. As we have seen, one of the major weaknesses of India's defence during even the Moghul period was that the imperial army had always to depend on foreigners for the casting of cannon.

It is an obvious fact that the industrial organization necessary to support a modern army has been becoming more and more complicated every day. Already in the nineteenth century it had become clear that an effective defence policy was possible only when it was supported by a stable society and a well-organized industrial system. The supremacy of Britain, France and Germany in the nineteenth century was based on the industrial predominance that these nations enjoyed. In recent years the unparalleled might of both the U.S.A. and the U.S.S.R. is based on the tremendous development of defence industries in both these countries. What created a widening gulf between past warfare and the warfare of the twentieth century was the invention of the internal combustion engine and its use in warfare. The internal combustion engine practically put the horse *hors de combat*. No more was the man on horseback invincible. Armies could be transported much more quickly in trucks than in horse-driven carriages or on horses. Light tanks were as manoeuvreable as cavalry and much faster. A mechanized army supported by tanks and with adequate air cover became an instrument of war which could only be opposed by armies similarly equipped. Now the most obvious fact about such an army was that it could be organized and maintained in the field only by a country with a most advanced industrial system behind it. The internal combustion engine requires not merely a variety of complicated skills but a highly developed industrial system to manufacture it successfully. To maintain such an industry in peacetime would be too much of a strain even for countries of medium size and reasonable resources. As is well known only a few of the more advanced countries of Europe have gone in for automobile production, not because they have not the technical competence to do it, but because such an industry cannot be maintained without a large enough internal market for its products.

The production of the internal combustion engine and the maintenance of an automobile industry manufacturing trucks, vehicles, light and heavy tanks, weapon carriers and all the other kinds of mechanized arms of war can only be the apex of an elaborate industrial system involving practically every aspect of industrial development. Without a powerful and extensive iron and steel industry it is not possible to undertake any major engineering works, far less the creation of an automobile industry. Heavy chemicals, aluminium, machine making industry, electronics, in fact all aspects of heavy and basic industries are closely connected with defence production and unless a country has developed its industrial potential sufficiently to meet its essential defence requirements, it could not undertake to protect its own interests.

The fact is, as General Fuller says: "A nation in arms demands a nation of armourers and technicians to sustain and maintain it. The nation which makes the greatest use of peace intervals to advance its mechanical and engineering potentials for war and which possesses the greatest number of skilled workers as well as trained soldiers, the most abundant supply of raw materials as well as arms, is the nation upon whom victory smiles." When Britain left India, the position was by no means happy. India's industrial development was lopsided. In none of the major spheres had her industry developed well enough to give adequate support to defence. Her steel industry, established for over 40 years (founded 1908), was producing barely a million tons of finished steel, insufficient even to meet her normal civilian demand. A small automobile industry had just come into being and had begun only to assemble the parts in India. So far as arms and equipment were concerned, Indian industry, apart from small arms and machine-guns produced in government arsenals, was unable to meet the defence requirements. In fact, the Indian army was dependent on British industrial strength for its existence as an efficient fighting arm.

There is a general idea that with the mechanization of the army, the number employed in defence services in times of war could be reduced. It is true that fewer men will be required to operate the destructive machines placed at the disposal of the armed forces. But the machines have to be produced; not merely produced and stockpiled but continuously improved upon and produced at a maximum rate once a war has started. The latest scientific discoveries have to be technologically exploited in terms of warfare, improvement in armaments, designs for new weapons, better and more powerful explosives. Further, effective answers to the enemy's discoveries have to be discovered and put into use. All this requires the mobilization of a very wide range of skills in the nation from top level scientists in the laboratory to skilled labourers in the factory. In fact, without widespread skills which could be mobilized to work in factories, the discoveries of scientists will not be available to the defence forces in time.

This weakness was not confined to defence research and industry only. India's position under the British was no better in respect of essential services like transport, power, fuel, etc. India had even before the second World War a fairly good railway system, but the locomotives had to come from England, and so to a very large extent also, the coaches. Power was but inadequately developed. So far as oil was concerned, apart from small quantities produced by the Assam Oil Company, India was almost wholly dependent on foreign supply.

Thus, looked at from every point of view, except that of manpower, India at the time of her independence was inadequately equipped for defence. She was dependent for almost every essential thing on Britain. What India's defence planners realized from the beginning was that no efficient military force could be built up for the defence of India, if everything essential for it had to be bought from outside. The most important thing was, therefore, to develop a defence industry freeing India from her dependence on others for her most necessary equipment. It was also realized that a defence industry could not be created independent of a national industrial system, and therefore the attempt was from the beginning to develop the industrial life of India from the bottom keeping in mind at the same time the necessities of defence. So, alongside with a general programme of industrialization India also tried to develop such essential units for defence like factories for testing prototypes, for manufacturing locomotives, army trucks and vehicles, and aeroplanes.

During the British period no serious effort had been made to develop the oil resources of India, mainly because, before the war, British requirements in this regard were amply met from Iran, Burma and Iraq. Independent India recognized that not only for civil purposes, but also for essential defence requirements, oil was a prime necessity. Here, as in some other spheres, she came up against the vested interests of American and British capital, which having immense oil interests in Iran, Iraq, Kuwait, Bahrein and Arabia were not altogether sympathetic to the Indian project of developing her own oil resources independently and through direct government investment. But with the technical assistance of the Soviet Union and Rumania, India has been able to make a beginning to develop her own oil resources.

Industrial development on the scale required for modern defence is dependent on the development of science and technology. The scientific basis of modern defence in all its aspects is something which the great leaders of war in the past centuries must find strange and surprising. Leadership, courage, physical stamina and other qualities which counted in battles and wars in the past do not count to the same extent now. As against a self-guided missile, these qualities have lost much of their glamour. But it is not only in respect of atomic weapons, guided missiles and nuclear war-heads that research has become important. There is in fact no arm of war where research has not reached the position of the highest importance. It is not only that every weapon can be improved by scientific research, that new and more deadly weapons can be invented, but that new defences have to be developed to counteract the effects of the enemies' inventions. This is obvious and unless a country is constantly improving its scientific research, its defence arrangements will fall behind those of others. The immense amount of money spent in defence research projects in advanced countries shows the importance they attach to scientific research. At the end of the Second War the position had become so clear that the then President of the Royal Society stated: "In any case is it not obvious that with the closing stages of this War, scientific discovery and inventions are becoming essential combatants. Science, an unwilling conscript, is becoming the undiscriminating devastation at long range, needing only a minimum of military apparatus or personnel — witness the German V weapons and now the atomic bomb."

In India this subject was taken up actively only after 1948. Then it was realized that the problem had to be looked at from two points of view; that of raising the general standard of scientific knowledge and research work in the country, and secondly, that of developing scientific research specifically in relation to defence problems. Without a much larger reservoir of scientific personnel and a more widespread diffusion of scientific knowledge and skill than India possessed it was not possible to create an adequate scientific background for defence. So from the early days of her independence India started on a bold and comprehensive policy in regard to scientific research. Attention was devoted no less to fundamental research than to applied research. Great national laboratories for research in physics, chemistry, electronics, in fact, in every field of pure science, were established with the object of providing facilities for research, as well as to widen the background of scientific knowledge. The net-work of new scientific centres that now exist all over the country bears witness to the importance that India attaches to the development of physical sciences.

Apart from this endeavour to create a genuine and widespread atmosphere of science and research, so essential for all aspects of national development, India has been devoting her attention specifically to scientific work in relation to defence matters. In 1948 an organization for scientific research in relation to defence problems was set up in Delhi and this service has since been functioning effectively as an essential part of India's defence establishment. The research problems that defence raises are widely different and extend from ballistics, explosives, radar, etc. to the reaction of human body to different temperatures and climates and to the nutritive value of rations. In fact there is no aspect of defence organization, from the human side of the forces to the utilization of the latest development of weapons, armament and protective devices, which does not fall under the purpose of scientific research.

India understood the importance of this work, but all that she has been able to do is to make a beginning and create a nucleus of scientific workers devoting themselves to the special problems of India's defence. The corps of Indian scientists is comparatively small. It has to be spread out to cover every kind of work which is of importance to the nation : research in pure science, in its application to industry, to technology, to human welfare and to defence. Though the resources which could be spared were not large, and the scientists who could be selected for this work were not many, the results which the organization has achieved so far have been significant. The evaluation of the efficiency of existing weapons, and the designing of new weapons, are important for all armies. Again ballistics, though of great significance at all times, has become specially important with the wider range of weapons which a defence force has at its disposal at the present time. Such highly complicated questions like the muzzle velocity of projectiles, the maximum pressure attained in the gun, the pressure time curve, are all important scientific problems in relation to arms which have constantly to be studied if, when the time comes, the army is not to be left with old-fashioned weapons. These can be checked and kept under constant examination only by scientists trained to a very high level of work.

The problems of research relating to the navy and air force are of course not the same. In both, a great deal of scientific work has to go into the construction of the types of vessels used, as they are continuously being improved. But so far as India is concerned these problems are in their infancy, for India is not yet ready to embark on large-scale schemes of naval or air construction. But there are other aspects of naval warfare where scientific research is of special importance to the Indian navy. The Naval Chemical and Metallurgical Laboratory in Bombay and the Indian Naval Physical Laboratory in Cochin are the two major units of research that India has built up during the last few years. This is of course apart from operational research on naval problems dealt with by the Defence Services Laboratory.

The special problems relating to the navy, which are the subject of research at the present time, deal with corrosion and anti-corrosion, physics of under-water sound, investigation of metallurgical failures. Knowledge of under-water sound is one of the essential requirements of naval operations. In these matters, as well as in such subjects as oceanography and marine survey, India is only at the start of her career in research.

But the important thing is that the Government realizes how essential it is to have scientists associated with army leaders at every stage of defence planning. Facilities are being created for this work : scientists are being trained and the defence forces are alive to their requirements, for they realize that no amount of courage and leadership would be sufficient to defend a country unless the defence forces are backed by the latest weapons and informed by the most up-to-date developments in science.

CHAPTER VIII

HAS INDIA THE NECESSARY RESOURCES FOR DEVELOPING AN ADEQUATE DEFENCE SYSTEM?

It is an obvious fact that a modern defence system can only be developed by countries possessing the necessary resources. The days when it was possible for small states heroically to defend their countries have passed away long ago. The armaments required for the military forces today could only be produced by highly industrialized nations having control over the raw materials necessary for industry. Beginning with coal and iron, defence industries require a wide variety of raw material, without which the essential requirements of the fighting forces from armaments to boots and buttons could not be produced. Mechanization requires an immense amount of fuel to keep the wheels of defence and of industry running. In the same manner, rubber has acquired a strategic importance which is almost unique. It is true that Germany conducted two great wars without any natural rubber and with but inadequate supply of natural petrol. But her science and industry were able to produce for her substitute materials of equal quality.

No country except perhaps the U.S.S.R. possesses all the resources for defence. Even she suffers from the weakness of not having access to suitable all-time ice-free ports. But apart from this natural deficiency, her more than continental character endows her with raw materials of every description in an ample measure. The United States is almost similarly placed—except perhaps in relation to rubber which can now be synthetically produced. Most other countries, however, suffer from some shortage of important materials essential for the purpose of defence and, therefore, have to stockpile them in times of peace.

So far as India is concerned she belongs on the whole to the fortunate category. The essential material requirements of an adequate defence system may be defined as follows :

1. An adequate supply of manpower of sufficient quality, physical stamina and courage.
2. Adequate space within which to organize and develop political and economic strength.
3. Availability under her own control of raw materials necessary for her defence industries.
4. A developed system of transportation, roads, railways, waterways, etc. through which goods and materials could move.

That India has adequate manpower resources of high quality need not be emphasized. Britain only partially exploited this manpower, confining recruitment to certain areas and to certain special groups. Experience of the last two wars has demonstrated that apart from these so-called martial classes, India possesses almost an inexhaustible supply of hardy and courageous fighters. The problem of manpower resources causes, therefore, no worry to India.

Equally from the point of view of size and space, India could be counted as being adequately endowed for the purpose of defence. How space is an important factor in defence has been proved time and again in history. Napoleon and Hitler in Russia, Japan in China are but recent and most convincing examples of this fact. Even the history of India provides ample proof of this doctrine. The Moghul empire, which was in relation to its time and area well organized for the purposes of war, took over a hundred years before its armies could claim mastery of the Deccan. Akbar started on his Deccan campaigns in the last decade of the sixteenth century. When Aurangzeb died, the Moghul armies were still fighting on the Tungabhadra. The armies that opposed the march of the Moghuls were not either from the point of view of discipline or of equipment comparable to the imperial forces ; but distance was a great factor. The more the imperial lines were extended the weaker became the offensive capacity of the armies.

The history of British conquest of India serves to emphasize the importance of space as a factor of defence. It took the British a full hundred years (from their first intervention in Arcot in 1748 to the second Sikh war in 1848) to conquer India. Many campaigns had to be fought and a continuous naval blockade of India enforced against foreign intervention before the British could claim to have established their authority over the territory of India.

Besides, though the Gangetic valley is one broad plain without physical features favourable to defence, the formidable Thar desert to the west and the mountainous Vindhya area to the south of the Ganges, Bundelkhand, Bagelkand and other hilly and forest areas provided excellent grounds for defensive warfare. In fact, in the period before the British these areas only acknowledged in name the sway of imperial dynasties. The Rajputana desert was never brought under occupation by the Muslim Sultans of Delhi before Akbar. It was by a political settlement — the Moghul-Rajput alliance — that even Akbar exercised his suzerainty over that area. From the moment that alliance was broken by Aurangzeb, Rajputana was a running sore to the empire. The wild forests and hilly areas of Bundelkhand tell the same tale. No power before the British was able to bring them effectively under control. It is also significant to remember that even the British chose to leave these two areas — Rajputana and Bundelkhand — under their own ancient rulers rather than try to bring them under direct administration.

The fact that the extent and varied physical features of India's territory contribute greatly to her capacity for defence is something which should never be overlooked. This is particularly important at the present time when the destructive capacity of bombs and weapons makes dispersal imperative. Under air bombardment, concentration of people, industries, administrative machinery in limited areas is dangerous and may lead to disaster. It is necessary in the interest of safety and security for these to be dispersed over as wide an area as possible. Where the extent of space available is limited, the effectiveness of destruction would obviously be the greatest. Though the Gangetic plain is overcrowded, India as a whole has extensive regions which are but thinly populated. Industry except to the extent necessitated by the concentration of national resources is already dispersed to a considerable extent. The necessities of defence have been kept in view in deciding on the location of industries so that there is no overwhelming concentration in a single area.

Thus the material resources for defence, it may be said, are there. But the question may well be asked whether in the light of past experience, the spiritual resources which are no less necessary for the effective defence of a people are strong at the present time. The first of these is the desire to remain free ; and to be ready for that purpose to make any sacrifice that one may be called upon to make. In the past, over considerable periods, this feeling was undoubtedly lacking in India. The sense of national unity had vanished and with it the sense of national freedom among many people and over wide areas. What was widely prevalent in the absence of national unity was a sense of regional or local patriotism which in many cases even worked against the freedom of India. Thus the Nawab of Oudh, for example, allied himself with the English East India Company for fear of the Mahrattas. The Rajput princes entered into feudatory relationships with the British in order to escape the authority of Scindia. The Raja of Travancore, rather than give in to the demands of the Mysore Ruler, made himself the servant of the foreigner. They were all patriots in their own limited way. Shuja-ud-Dowla of Oudh who made the alliance with the East India Company was one of the shrewdest statesmen of the time. He desired to save Oudh from the Mahrattas. Though the titular Wazir of the empire of India, he had no conception of Indian unity and no vision of Indian freedom. This was the position with other leaders also. The eighteenth century was in fact a time when fissiparous tendencies had taken full possession of the Indian political scene.

It was not only the dynasts and men of ambition that had lost the sense of patriotism but the common people. There was no sense of loyalty even to the regional rulers, as they for the most part, like the Nawab of Arcot in the Carnatic, the Nizam in Hyderabad, and the Naib Nazim in Bengal, represented no principle of authority beyond that of usurpation. In the more ancient principalities, no doubt a sense of deep loyalty to the monarch was always present. Also in what was in the circumstances of the time, national states, like the Mahratta empire at Poona, and the Sikh kingdom of Lahore, there was an intense sense of patriotism, but broadly in the eighteenth century a sense of loyalty to the nation and the determination to remain free had disappeared from India. The peasants and traders in Bengal did not feel that they had lost their freedom when they exchanged the rule of Naib Nazim for the government of the East India Company.

Is the position fundamentally changed today and if so how strong is the feeling of Indian unity? This is a question which has to be carefully analyzed and understood if the problem of India itself is to be understood. Undoubtedly, there are, if viewed from outside, many divisive tendencies in India. It is a country of many languages, each claiming the passionate loyalty of millions. It is also a country with many sub-nationalities with long historical traditions of which they are proud. In fact, there is no area in India which does not claim primacy in some respect or another. Magadha was the homeland of the early empires and the birth place of Jainism and Buddhism — in fact it was the great empire-state of ancient India. But the Kalingas do not yield the pride of place and claim to have a parallel historical tradition strengthened by overseas achievements. The Andhras have besides significant claims to imperial title the unique distinction of having contributed effectively to the integration of the North with the South. So with every part of India. But it is significant to remember that though each claims a distinction in respect of its neighbours that distinction is within the framework of India's history and in relation to India's evolution. The claim is not based on separatism but is one of emphasis as local characteristics. In the absence of a central government these factors may become important but in the context of the world today when the tendency is towards the evolution of larger political units, the political unity of India seems safe enough from the challenge of its own divisive tendencies.

Besides, the old doctrine of *swadharma* which in all periods of history strongly moved the Indian people adds a binding element to the Indian nationhood of today. There is no denying the fact that the solid basis on which the imposing structure of India's nationhood is raised is the Hindu Reformation of the nineteenth and the first half of the twentieth centuries. That movement which purged Hinduism of the accretions of centuries, abolished untouchability, undermined caste, provided equality of status for women, purified the temples and revivified the doctrines of Hinduism is something which has provided a new dynamism in the Hindu people. The *swadharma* of the Hindus today is something vital, progressive and adapted to the needs of the time. By that purification, the essential fact that the people of India, who became integrated into a community in the centuries before Christ, continue today as an important factor in the world, has become obvious to all. The Hindu people who were the contemporaries of ancient Egypt and Babylon and later of Greece, Rome and China continue to be the contemporaries of the U.S.A. and the U.S.S.R. This sense of continuity and of an indestructible *dharma* which, however overlaid in the past with superstitions, false creeds and reactionary dogmas, stands out again as an inspiring guidance, is something which gives to Indian nationhood a feeling of permanence and strength.

Nor does this emphasis on revived Hinduism affect the lay and secular character of the state. In a country of four hundred million people over three hundred and forty million continue to be Hindus. There is no area where they are not in a large majority. Besides, the identification of the Hindu people with India is not only historical but also cultural. When we talk of Indian music, dance, architecture, literature, it is basically the contribution of the Hindu people to the world culture that is indicated. The contribution of the minority groups has no doubt enriched this heritage but no one would deny that culturally India remains predominantly Hindu.

The fissiparous tendencies are more apparent than real not merely because the strength of Hinduism unites all the parts but the conditions of the twentieth century clearly demonstrate that the economic and political structure of the nuclear age can only be on the basis of large units. The economic reconstruction now being undertaken in India is beyond the capacity of any one of the states of the federation, large enough though most of them be in relation to many European states. The size of the Soviet Union extending from the Ukranian plains to the Pacific and from the Arctic Ocean to the Pamirs and the frontiers of Persia, of the United States covering half a continent, of China with a population of 650 millions, and the efforts of the Western European nations to achieve political unity burying the rivalries of the past, are sufficient to demonstrate that political organizations, to survive as independent units in the present age, have to build on the widest foundation. India, though partitioned at the time of her independence, achieved this basis when she was able to persuade the princely states to integrate with her and to build a federal state giving equal opportunity to all parts.

The units have, therefore, a sense of loyalty to the Union which they did not possess before. The defence of

Kashmir is felt by the people of Kerala as being no less important than the protection of their own coastline. What is even more significant is that participation in a democratic political life, where every one has equal freedom and equal rights without the sense of being oppressed by any community or by any region, has given to the people a pride in their nationhood which extends to a wider circle than at any other time. The pride of independent nationhood and free democratic life is strong enough to overcome the petty feelings of jealousy and rivalry based on language and regionalism.

The basic problem of defence in modern society is national integration. In spite of appearances it seems clear that India's integration has proceeded sufficiently for her to face any danger without the fear of the structure falling apart. The creation of linguistic units providing ample scope for regional patriotism has especially strengthened India's integration.

The fear once entertained by many faint-hearted theorists that provinces based on languages will strengthen the forces of separatism and may endanger the unity of India has been proved to be wholly wrong. On the other hand, the experiment of yoking together communities living in separate geographical areas and speaking well-developed languages has proved to be a source of weakness. A sense of national integration based on healthy regional rivalries, with the Centre representing the varied life of the country, is the best guarantee of the Indian Union.

Also, the strains of defence in a normal society help to bind the population together ; Pakistan's intervention in Kashmir was in this sense a great stimulant to India's integration. Not only did the fact of having to fight Pakistan in Kashmir help to cement the feeling of nationhood at a difficult time, but the apparent danger to India helped to make India defence-minded as she had never been before. The Hyderabad incident had also the same result. Hyderabad in the belly of India, which except for its Muslim dynasty was more Indian than most areas, was threatened with a Razakar rising which challenged the unity of India. This challenge also did not fail to cement the integration already achieved for the Muslims in India stood solidly with the rest of the country in the police action that followed. Then again recently, the evidence of a Chinese challenge to the Indian boundaries on the outer side of the Himalayas brought to the surface the sense of Indian nationhood more than perhaps anything else. Events in Ladakh, in areas which even educated people had not heard of, moved the population to an extent that came as a surprise to most people.

These facts have demonstrated the strength of India's nationhood in a striking way and the fear that many people once entertained that India's political integration was fragile and would break to pieces when it faced any danger has been seen to be illusory.

The desire to be free is there. The sense of national unity is undoubtedly strong now. But will India develop fast enough her resources of defensive strength to be able to stand alone? This requires a much wider circle of national efficiency, an educated population, a sense of political stability and a social integration which could stand the shock of successive crises. Without a wider circle of national efficiency, prolonged defence will not be possible ; without an educated population the danger of national values being forgotten will be there in times of danger ; without political stability leadership will be weak and may even break down ; without strong social integration the external strains may lead to internal revolution. History provides ample and awful examples to prove these conclusions. Absence of a wider circle of national efficiency led to the defeat of Japan which could not compete with her enemies in material production. The absence of an educated population which could give strength to national defence led in the past to the break-down of most Indian kingdoms when they faced grave external danger. The failure of political stability led to the down-fall of France in 1940. The weaknesses of Russia's internal integration led to the October Revolution of 1917. India realizes these dangers to her unity.

A widening standard of national efficiency is something which India is consciously striving to achieve. That can only come from all round progress: economic, industrial, scientific and above all educational. The recognition of this fact is at the bottom of India's successive Five Year Plans and her emphasis on a rapid technological advance through science. Her social reorganization, apart from its human values, has also the same objective, that of strengthening the bonds of her social life against the possibility of disintegration. These are the true sources of defensive strength, and these India has been cultivating to some extent in order to achieve her independence and much more in order to defend it.

When a country neglects these factors of its defence, however strong materially it may be, it may fail when it comes against equally strong forces. This is an axiomatic proposition which requires no proof to establish its validity. In India this process of broadening the circle of national efficiency, of accelerating industrial advancement, scientific growth and other basic necessities of defence are of recent origin and unless they are steadily pursued, our inherent weaknesses will assert themselves, making us a prey to any aggression.

CHAPTER IX

INDIA'S NAVAL DEFENCE

DURING THE last twelve years, India has been trying to build up a navy for the defence of her shores. But the question has often been asked whether in view of the heavy expenditure involved, the inability of India to build her own ships and the fact that the ships which constitute her navy are mostly second-hand and do not conform to the requirements of today, the effort has been worth the while. Does a small navy fulfil any serious function of defence in the changed circumstances of today? Is it not better for India to depend on her land and air power to defend her shores? These questions raise important principles. What constitutes a small navy is a matter of comparison ; so is the outmoded character of ships. The Iraqi navy consists of four patrol vessels and a yacht. The Ceylon navy is also of a similar character. They are no doubt symbolic and are useful for dealing with smugglers and for undertaking other similar duties. In comparison with these, the Indian navy consisting of an aircraft carrier, two cruisers, destroyers, corvettes, etc. is a powerful force. Nor can the ships of the Indian navy be considered as being out of date or of limited use in warfare except in relation to the navies of a great power. In fact, in relation to the states in her neighbourhood, the Indian navy cannot be considered a small navy or her ships outmoded. Except in comparison with the navies of U.S.A., U.S.S.R., Britain and France, the Indian navy, as it is constituted, is a force of considerable strength and significance.

It is undoubtedly true that the navy is even more dependent than land forces on equipment of all sorts. The variety of naval units has itself become great. The complexity of their construction increases day by day. They have to carry all kinds of complicated instruments. For example, anti-submarine warfare which began with simple depth charges has evolved such a variety of complicated machinery such as listening gear, electronic soncers, and homing torpedoes. The navy has in fact become the most technical of services.

All this makes even small units highly expensive. Units like a medium-sized cruiser, not to speak of an aircraft carrier, are outside the financial capacity of small nations. A large navy with the necessary compliment of aircraft carriers, cruisers, destroyers, submarine craft and other auxiliary vessels is clearly beyond India's capacity for at least two or three decades to come. But that is a problem which need not concern us as in terms of her regional interests she does not require a navy of that type or that quality. Her immediate interest is the defence of her coastline in terms of the powers in her neighbourhood. Her naval requirements have therefore to be considered in terms of their resources, individually and in combination. So long as the Indian navy is organized adequately to meet and to overcome any dangers from powers near to her coastline, her immediate purpose may be said to have been served.

In spite of India having a long coastline, the problem of naval defence forced itself upon her only after her independence. Till 1922, the question was not considered at all as the British navy was supreme on the seas and there seemed to be no power strong enough at the time to challenge it seriously. The attempt of Germany to enter the Persian Gulf by the backdoor had been thwarted. France was not a considerable naval power, at least so far as the East was concerned. Japan had built up her naval strength under the protection of the Anglo-Japanese alliance and the British were inclined to look upon the Empire of the Rising Sun, at least till the first years of the war of 1914–18, with a mixture of patronage and sympathy. The elimination of Germany seemed to strengthen Britain's position. To the outside observer India's naval defences under the auspices of the British navy seemed more secure than even before.

But new factors had come into existence. During the discussions on the Treaty of Peace at Versailles, the wrangle over Guam and Yap and the Japanese claims in the Pacific showed that Japan had entered the naval race in seriousness; and that America was standing forth as a claimant to the supremacy of the seas. The Washington Conference on the limitation of naval armaments, which was called on the initiative of the United States, decided on a world ratio of 5 : 5 : 3 as between America, Britain and Japan. This gave Japan at least a naval parity in the Pacific and the Far East. The position of the British navy in regard to the defence of India had to be reconsidered and consequently, as we have seen, a beginning was made for the creation of an Indian navy.

At the time of withdrawal of the British, India thus had the nucleus of a navy. Unlike the army it was no more than a subsidiary arm. Such as it was, it had also to be partitioned, and the flotilla of destroyers, frigates and mine-sweepers, which formed the major portion of the navy, was divided in the same proportion as the army was. What was left to India were four sloops, two frigates, one corvette, twelve mine-sweepers, four tankers, and a few auxiliary vessels. So far as training

8

establishments were concerned gunnery, radar, tactical navigation schools and the Boys' Training Establishment went to Pakistan. So practically speaking India had to begin almost from scratch. But at the time of independence, Britain had made it clear that she would help India in every way to build up an independent navy, to give training and instruction to Indian naval officers, to assist India to establish her training centres — in fact to cooperate wholeheartedly to create a navy suited to India's requirements. This obligation she has fulfilled most generously, supplying suitable vessels — destroyers, cruisers and an aircraft carrier — training the necessary personnel for manning these ships, helping in the establishment of training institutions in India, taking a number of officers in the higher naval training centres in Britain and finally by allowing the Indian navy to participate with British units in naval exercises in Indian waters.

The last twelve years have seen the Indian navy grow from small beginnings to an important task force. True, it is not, and will not be for some time, a naval force capable by itself of undertaking the defence of India's long coastline against a major naval power. Nor is such a navy today required by India. As we have emphasized more than once, India's preparations are not in terms of defending herself single-handed adequately against a great power but in relation to the states of her own region. In the conditions of what may be called a limited local war her strength is adequate to defend her coasts, to protect her trade, and to maintain her communications. In case she has to participate in a war of major proportions in alliance with others the role of her navy will be to guard her own area and to participate with the naval forces of her allies.

Compared to the strength of the states washed by the Indian Ocean, the Indian navy is a powerful instrument of defence. Beyond this India does not desire to go, especially as the nature of future naval formations, in view of the power of the air arm and of recent developments in weapons, cannot be foreseen now. Is the navy of the future mainly going to the based on under-water units? Would the surface craft, especially the aircraft carrier and the cruiser, continue to have a dominant position as they did during the second World War? The Soviet Union is said to have scrapped a large proportion of her surface crafts and is reported to be building an overwhelmingly powerful under-sea fleet. In Britain itself recent changes in naval construction have been revolutionary. She seems to have thrown on the scrap heap many of the cherished ideas of former times and is now concentrating on new types in order to meet the changed circumstances.

It is of course obvious that especially in the case of the navy, fighting units must be continually adjusted to the armament which could be brought up by the enemy. The danger of attack from the air led to the construction of giant aircraft carriers which could give round-the-clock air protection to the ships. In the same way the possibility of attack by weapons with nuclear war-heads would lead to the construction of other types of vessels, possibly under-sea craft which could remain submerged for a long time. Under the British Five Year Defence Plan (1957–62) the emphasis is on guided missile ships with specially compact propelling machinery, carrying the Sea Slug missiles for long-range interception of aircraft, and the sea craft missiles for close air defence. Similarly, every type of naval craft has been designed to meet the changed circumstances. When the reorganized navy assembles for review in 1962 it would present a totally different spectacle to what the world has been accustomed to see.

Though the reforms are radical and farsighted, how far could they be said to be the final form of naval construction, at least for a short-term period of ten to fifteen years? So far as India is concerned, there is no question now of her undertaking to build a navy for the nuclear age. For at least a decade or two to come her navy will be confined to conventional fighting units, like cruisers, destroyers, frigates, etc. With the support of one or two aircraft carriers, backed by an adequate naval air arm, her own limited purposes would be adequately served.

The present weaknesses of Indian naval defence relate mainly to three factors. In the first place, India has so far developed no submarine flotilla. Nor has she adequate training facilities for submarine warfare. It is an undisputed fact that, for the future, under-sea craft will achieve much greater importance in naval warfare than at any time in the past. Mr. Krushchev himself in a note to President Eisenhower has gone to the extent of declaring that " the heyday of surface navy power is over. In the age of nuclear and rocket weapons these formidable warships are fit for nothing but for courtesy visits, gun salutes and as targets for rockets." Though this statement may be wholly true only in the case of a state like the Soviet Union which is independent of maritime communications, either for trade or for the defence of its own territory, few will deny the immensely increased importance of the submarine in the warfare of the future. It can now remain submerged for much longer periods. It can carry and deliver light nuclear war-heads. As a recent writer has said: "The marriage of a relatively simple nuclear armed missile to the most stealthy and hidden of naval craft has created . . . the ballistic missile submarine." Besides, from small-sized craft they have now become under-sea ships of considerable size capable of functioning as army transport. In fact, there is no reason to doubt that, just as airborne invasions are now a regular part of warfare, in the next stage why submarine borne invasions should not present a major threat.

All this clearly demonstrates that though the shape of the navy to come, even for the next decade, has by no means been finally settled, submarine warfare will become more and more important. In the circumstances, no country can afford to neglect it. Of course it would not be possible for India for financial no less than other reasons to embark on a programme of acquiring a sufficient number of submarines to add to her fleet. Nor can she, for at least another two decades to come, manufacture her own craft. But that does not mean that she should not build up the nucleus of a submarine flotilla, utilize it not only for the purpose of training but of research into problems connected with submarine warfare and with the designing and construction of this type of ships.

Secondly, India is almost wholly dependent on other countries for the supply of ships for the navy. Her shipbuilding capacity in modern terms is only at a beginning stage and in the matter of warships she has made but a modest start by constructing in her own shipyards a mine-sweeper and a survey ship. Though the navy has a branch which is concerned with designing and construction, there is no prospect in the immediate future of India building major units for her own navy. Apart from the short supply of steel plates, special alloys and other requirements, it will take considerable time before Indian engineers acquire the skill to design and construct men-of-war. This means that India will at least for some years to come be dependent on other nations for the supply of ships to her navy.

That the weakness of building a navy on acquired ships makes continued improvements difficult and replacement costly, need not be emphasized. It is not too much to say that unless a country builds its own ships, continuously modifies them to suit changed circumstances, and plans in terms of what its neighbours and rivals are doing, its naval defence can never be effective. In this way it is different from the army. The army fighting on solid ground can put up with many irregularities ; but a navy cannot fight on leaking ships or engage with units of superior speed and fire power. Unless, therefore, India follows a policy leading her, within a measurable period, to the position of being able to design and build the ships of her own navy, her defence from the naval point of view will always be weak.

These are in some measure remediable factors, dependent upon India's industrial growth and scientific research. But her third weakness is something more difficult to overcome. The seas that wash her shores are not closed or regional seas like the Baltic, the North Sea, the Aegean, or the Sea of Japan, which could be defended easily from strategic points. The Arabian Sea and the Bay of Bengal open out into the Indian Ocean and entry into these seas is not commanded from any point. True, from the Pacific the entry through the straits of Malacca can be controlled from Singapore or the Nicobars. In the same way, the entry into the Arabian Sea from the Red Sea can be controlled from Aden and the Babel Mandeb. But these are of lesser importance compared to the straight route to India's coast from the south where the wide open oceans meet without any cover from land.

Nor is the coastline itself provided with a protective cover of islands. The west coast of India has only a reef of coral atolls, the Laccadives, which afford no protection from the enemy, and do not provide even an adequate air and naval base. The whole coastline from Cape Comorin to Kutch is exposed and can be protected only by the superior might of the navy.

The situation is slightly different in respect of the Bay of Bengal. Here the Andaman and Nicobar Islands, extending almost to the mouth of the straits of Malacca, can provide both air and naval bases sufficiently advanced to give a protective cover to the coast. But even here, though the protection may be adequate for any approach through the straits of Malacca, it is difficult to cover the opening from the south.

The basic fact is that no naval defence is effective without advance bases and in this matter India is unfortunately placed. The importance of this consideration was not fully recognized during the British period as the strategic points of defence, Singapore, Aden, Trincomalee, the ports of the African coast, were all in British hands. Today the situation is different. The guarding of India's coastline can be undertaken only if the navy has a powerful air arm, and an adequate number of aircraft carriers, which could constantly patrol the area in times of crisis.

Similar difficulties exist with regard to the air force. So far, the Indian air force has been conceived as a subordinate arm of the defence forces, meant to give air support to the army. But it is obvious that in the future it has a more positive role to play than to give support to ground forces. In the circumstances of India, the air arm has to cooperate closely with the navy if the coasts of India have to be protected. The protection of the navy itself will be to a large extent dependent upon giant aircraft carriers from which the air could be patrolled, enemy's ships bombed and the sea lanes for India's commerce protected. Even now without a powerful air arm to support it, the navy loses much of its effectiveness. Here also the main problem that troubles us is India's industrial and scientific backwardness. No doubt India is now beginning to manufacture under licence different kinds of aircraft for the air force. But without a parallel development of scientific research, India will not be able to give her air force the most up-to-date aircraft with necessary equipment for defensive and offensive purposes.

Briefly, from the point of view of naval and air defence what stands in the way, even more than in the case of the army, is our weakness in industry and our backwardness in science. In these two arms, the primary requirement is the quality of the machine or the ships, the armament and other equipment. On borrowed science defence cannot flourish, as Japan discovered in the second World War. She could not improve on the Zero fighter with which she started the war, while the Americans were putting better and newer models in the air. Nor could she build naval units as fast and as efficiently as the Americans were able to do. The comparative backwardness of her industrial and scientific position ensured her defeat.

India's position no doubt is different, as she does not envisage a war with one of the great powers, but defence has, at all times, taken into consideration the best and not the next best, which depend on science and technical advancement.

CHAPTER X

FOREIGN POLICY AND INTERNAL STRUCTURE IN RELATION TO DEFENCE

THE INTEGRAL relation between foreign policy and defence is obvious enough and requires no proof to establish it. The purpose of foreign policy is primarily to safeguard the independence of the state and the sanction behind is the organized strength of the state. The safety and the security of a state and its life as an independent unit are dependent on the capacity of its armed forces to defend it. But with the best army a country can still be ruined if its policy follows wrong lines. The armed forces fight the enemy in the field; but the political conditions under which the army fights, its alliances, enmities, ambitions, etc. are the outcome of a country's policy. A country which enters into a war without adequate diplomatic preparation and continues to fight, however bravely, without parallel activities in the diplomatic field, ensures its own defeat. Allies have to be secured and strengthened and enemies have to be weakened; those who are unfriendly should at least be made neutrals. The experience of Germany in the two wars should help to emphasize the importance of foreign policy in matters relating to defence; especially would this be clear if the history of the two previous German wars, the Prusso-Austrian and the Franco-German wars of 1865 and 1870, were examined. In the two latter cases, Bismark had by a masterly foreign policy secured the neutrality of other powers and was, therefore, able to bring his campaigns to successful conclusions. In the first Great War, however, Germany and Austria, though when the war started were opposed only by Britain, France and Russia, ended by having practically the whole world ranged against them. It was not the defence forces that failed but Germany's foreign policy. Similar was the position in the second World War also.

We have already noticed that the British in India developed their defence in full coordination with a carefully considered foreign policy. From the time of Warren Hastings a policy had been evolved in relation to the Country Powers, the essential purpose of which was to safeguard the security of the East India Company's possessions. But after Wellesley, when the dominant authority in India had passed to the British, the security of the whole of India became their concern. Consequently, a foreign policy in the proper sense of the term, the purpose of which was to ensure the safety of the country, was formulated and put into effect. The attack on Tipu was justified by Wellesley on the ground that the Ruler of Mysore was in correspondence with the French whose presence in Egypt Wellesley considered a menace to the safety of the British interests in India. The Malcolm Mission to Persia was, as we have already pointed out, a measure of defence against the Franco-Russian agreement at Tilsit. During the middle of the century, with the advance of the Czar's empire into Central Asia, a new objective comes into Indian defence policy : to keep the Russian power as far away from the frontiers of India by erecting and supporting a buffer state between them. The partition of Persia into zones of influence and the neutralization of Afghanistan were parts of British India's grand strategy of defence. In fact in the period from 1885 to 1914, the British Indian Government followed a consistent policy of creating an iron fence around India in the form of buffer states as a part of the defence arrangements of India. The occupation of Egypt was justified on the ground of safeguarding communications with India. The protectorate over the sheikhs and sultans of the Persian and Trucial coasts had originally the same object of safeguarding India's security. Similarly, Tibet and Siam (Thailand) during this period became the subject of British diplomatic and other activity for the purpose of safeguarding the security of India. In these matters, policy was the handmaid of defence.

But it has to be remembered that foreign policy, however wisely conceived and ably followed up, would not be able to achieve any success if it had no adequate military strength to back it. The ultimate and decisive factor in diplomacy is the strength which backs it. The question which Stalin is said to have asked about the Papacy, how many battalions the Pope had behind him, is valid in respect of temporal powers, though it is not obviously applicable to forces which depend on higher values. The most valiant diplomatic efforts of a country, which is powerless to defend itself and is a prey to the pressure of any predatory state, can lead to no effective results. In fact, foreign policy and strength in defence are mutually dependent.

Clausewitz, the greatest of military thinkers, declared that war is the continuation of policy, that is to say, that force is resorted to when policy has failed to yield results. The objective is to secure something which policy has defined and considered to be necessary. As war therefore is not an object in itself, but only a method of obtaining results by compelling the enemy to yield to superior force, the problems of declaring war and making peace—not necessarily the conduct of war — have to be subordinate to political considerations.

The conduct of war in the field is the business of the generals. The conduct of war at the higher levels of strategy has necessarily to be in the hands of those who determine policy, and must take into consideration political factors, the interests of allies and neutrals, future relationships with the enemy, the most fruitful utilization of available resources, etc. Briefly, defence, in its active functioning, is not a matter solely for the army. The history of every war of which we have knowledge proves the fact that unless policy is rightly defined and carefully executed, war as a measure of enforcement must necessarily fail though battles may be won and victories claimed.

If foreign policy is thus an essential aspect of defence, internal policies have often as decisive an effect in shaping the outcome of wars. The defence organization of a country rent by internal divisions and lacking political unity or social solidarity can never be effective especially in modern times when warfare is not confined to ranged battle between armies. Social integration and political solidarity are, therefore, essential conditions of successful defence. Of these, social integration is of greater basic importance. The fate of the Austrian and Ottoman empires during the first World War should help to prove this fact. Before the war, though both were comparatively powerful states, owing to their supranational character, no social integration had been achieved among their diverse population. The Czechs, the Serbs, the Croats, the Poles and other national groups in the old Austro-Hungarian empire had no bond of union beyond a common ruler. The consequence was that under the pressure of a modern war, the ramshackle empire of the

Hapsburgs broke up into many parts. The position of the Ottoman empire was very similar. Though the empire had existed over five hundred years, no social integration had been achieved between the different peoples of the empire. The Turks, a minority except in Anatolia, ruled over a conglomeration of races. The Arabs, the Armenians, the Kunds and other peoples of the empire thus became a source of weakness. When, after the war, Turkey was reconstituted, Mustafa Kamal Ata Turk was wise enough to insist that the new state should be socially integrated in order to build up its strength to defend its frontiers.

The lack of integration in these two empires that led to extreme weakness in defence arose from racial differences. They are the most obvious cases of internal conflict. Besides, there are other, perhaps too obvious, sources of social conflict even in apparently well integrated societies arising, for example, from the oppression of one class by another, persecution of a religious sect by a dominant group, too great an imbalance in the distribution of wealth, etc. Many instances could be adduced from early times when defence had been weakened by these factors. In our times what is known as fifth column activities inside the enemy's country —meant to weaken his *morale*, reduce his fighting power, etc. — are based on these factors. The propaganda of the enemy which has now become a major arm in warfare owing to the possibility of reaching directly the enemy public over the head of governments, is naturally directed against such weaknesses. The last two wars especially demonstrated this. Naturally, governments under pressure of wartime circumstances make fair promises both to their own people and to the peoples of enemy countries. During the first World War, Great Britain found it necessary to compromise with Indian nationalism, to promise freedom to the Irish and in England itself to introduce universal franchise, votes for women and a more just social order. To the enemy peoples perhaps the promises made had the essential object of getting them to rise against their own governments. The promise of liberation to the Arabs, of freedom and independence to the subject nationalities of the Austro-Hungarian empire etc., show how the Allies exploited the internal weaknesses of their enemies. Nor did Germany fail to play a similar game. They were loud in their protestations of sympathy to the Irish. They set up in Berlin a provisional Government of India in 1915. During the second World War these activities were even more pronounced. Not a little of the credit for the rapid success of Japan in her campaign in South-East Asia was due to the exploitation of the internal weakness of her enemies. In Indo-China, Thailand, the Philippines, Indonesia, Malaya and Burma, the Japanese were able to play upon local sentiments against the Western nations who, except in Thailand, enjoyed complete political authority and were thus able to undermine the defensive capacity of the ruling colonial governments.

In future wars it is obvious that the method of undermining defence will be more extensively followed as the machinery of propaganda has been improved to a greater extent than even before. Besides this direct undermining of morale by positive propaganda, nations have at all times used also other methods to frighten the enemies and weaken their will to resist. Both Ganghiz Khan and Taimur were expert in this line. Long before they attacked a country they used to spread rumours about the terror-striking capacity of their armies, how ferocious they were, how pyramids of heads were raised in the areas which they conquered. By these means, they used to undermine the morale of the countries they attacked.

All these methods show how important social and political integration is for the proper defence of a country. If the country is easily to be frightened into taking measures in haste, without proper consideration or coordination of overall strategy, the enemy wins half the battle. War hysteria is, therefore, one of the most dangerous weaknesses which could affect a sound policy of defence. To prevent such hysteria or even war psychosis developing in a nation should be a major point of national policy. Proper defence measures have to be the outcome of careful thinking in peacetime and not hasty improvisation in response to hysterical national demands. Therein lies the importance of defence planning on a continuing basis.

A plan that has been drawn up has to be continuously adjusted not only to changed conditions of warfare, weapons, etc., but also to developing political conditions. In the case of India, for example, all previous plans of defence had to be reconsidered in view of the changed conditions in Tibet. Not only had defence plans to be adjusted but organizational changes in the army structure had also to be carefully studied in view of the differences in terrain, climate and other conditions of the area. For defence in the plains, the army formations required today are mechanized and quick moving, with concentrated fire power and capable, where necessary, of offering battle. For fighting in mountain areas of over twelve thousand feet, covered with snow, the type of formations would clearly have to be different. Mechanized transport may be difficult in the absence of a settled population. In any case, the mere logistics of operations in the Himalayan areas would necessitate light armed alpine units, each one small but working in coordination. This method of adjustment of planning to changing circumstances requires careful and continued study. Any hasty improvisation may lead to disaster.

Political hysteria is, therefore, a menace to the proper planning of defence. Warfare today is directed as much against social stability and economic and industrial production as against armies in the field. Consequently, defence involves the creation and operation of machinery to safeguard the internal structure of the nation and to prevent it from succumbing to any propaganda. This is not a part of the army's functions but of the civil government which not merely has the duty to uphold the morale of the nation but also to weaken and, if possible, to break the morale of the enemy. This is by no means a new development. In the *Mahabharata*, Krishna proclaims that one of the objects of his visit to the Kaurava Court was to expound the righteousness of the Pandava claims and to expose the injustice of the Kaurava stand. This was so successfully achieved that until today we judged the leader in the Kaurava-Pandava struggle in terms of the war propaganda embodied in the epic, though there are other passages which throw a different light on the main actors. In fact, it may well be said that with the invention of radio and other methods of mass communication, which can be operated over the heads of governments, propaganda addressed directly to the people and meant to undermine the morale of the enemy has become a major factor in warfare.

One other factor may also be emphasized as affecting the moral basis of defence : and that is the creation of a conviction, in the minds of the people, that what they are defending are essential principles of morality and justice. It is Napoleon who said that the moral factor in war is as two-thirds to one-third. The conviction that your interests are mixed up with the general good is an important factor in the morale of civilized men. Thus slogans such as "war to end war" and "war to make democracy safe", and President Wilson's idealistic proclamations were important in creating in the minds of the masses the basic conviction of the rightness of the cause for which they were making unheard of sacrifices. Defence of one's own country is indeed a great and unimpeachable objective: people will at all times willingly suffer every kind of sacrifices and fight with fanaticism for ideals and for ideological considerations more than even for selfish interests. The fanaticism with which the crusades and the wars of religion were fought was much more intensive than anything which patriotism could evoke. Today if religion does not evoke the same feeling, other ideas and ideologies have taken its place. During the last two World Wars, these ideas had to be consciously formulated, e.g., the Atlantic Charter and national emotions worked up around them in order to secure the solidarity necessary for so prolonged a conflict.

This is an aspect of modern warfare which requires close attention. It is *swadharma* that has the greatest appeal in India. It is a wide enough concept to include all interests in the country and indeed to be universal. It has also, in spite of its universalism, a special local emphasis which helps to identify it with the ideal that India stands for. A continuous and widening interpretation of *swadharma* is a necessary condition of India's defence policy.

CONCLUSION

As an ancient country which has become newly independent, India's defence problems present a combination of old and new factors. The social and political structures of India determine the structure of her defence forces, the composition of her officer cadre and the relationship of the forces to the public. The changed political circumstances of the present time which are closely related to her own independence, create for her, new problems of defence like those arising from the partition of the subcontinent into India and Pakistan, and the even more significant development of a highly organized military state across the Himalayas. With the protective arm of the British fleet considerably weakened in the Indian Ocean, a new frontier of defence, formerly closed for over one hundred years, has also been opened. India has to face these problems, with her industrial potential still undeveloped and her scientific skills on which much of the modern defence depends still in a backward state. Also, by a decision of high policy she decided to deal with her own problems without the protective support of military alliances with more powerful states.

Why has India denied herself the benefits of an alliance with more powerful states at a time when even great powers like England have found it necessary to join offensive and defensive alliances in order to safeguard their interests? Britain is a member of the Atlantic Pact, of the Baghdad Pact (now C.E.N.T.O.), of the

S.E.A.T.O., thus in effect covering her position all over the world. She is allied with America, France and her European friends, with the Muslim states of Turkey, Iran and Pakistan, with the South-East Asian states of Thailand and the Philippines. Similar in a way is the position of France. If two of the great powers who held the international stage for over two centuries could thus ally themselves with stronger and weaker nations what reason is there for India to stand apart and refuse to ally herself with any state or group of states?

To understand this, one has to go back to Indian history. It was through " subordinate alliances " for the purpose of defending their territories that the rulers of India lost their independence in the late eighteenth and the first half of the nineteenth century. By calling in a stronger power to help you in defending your independence, you subordinate your policies to the advice of the protecting power and thereby limit your independence. Inevitably, though perhaps after the lapse of a certain time, the stronger ally becomes the major partner, reducing the weaker partner to the position of a satellite. Thus an alliance between states, which are not mutually dependent, but one of which is very much stronger while the other seeks its support for protection, leads to the subordination of the weaker partner. From the time of the Confederation of Delos to our own day, this has been the experience and this was the process by which India lost her independence in the eighteenth and the first half of the nineteenth century.

With so recent an experience to warn her it is not surprising that India has refused to allow herself to be allied in mutual security pacts. Besides, the influence of strong nations on the internal structure of their weaker allies has also appeared to India to be disastrous. The sense of ultimate responsibility for defence, a strong motive force at all times for the development of national unity and hard work, itself becomes weakened by the feeling of dependence on the strength of others. Internally, a government dependent on outside help loses authority and prestige as experience in many of the countries allied in this manner has demonstrated. Moreover the stronger partner, however much he may desire to follow a policy of absolute non-intervention in internal affairs, is forced by his own interest often to advice, and sometimes even to intervene in the affairs of his ally. In the case of a powerful nation, the reaction which follows such intervention, open or concealed, would be strong. The instance of the Anglo-American Good Offices Mission in the recent Franco-Tunisian dispute would illustrate this. Neither America nor England was anxious to intervene or even to offer mediation in the Franco-Tunisian dispute. But as peace in the Mediterranean was a major allied interest, they offered their good offices to settle the controversy. But the sensitiveness of France was such that when the public realized that her major allies were in effect intervening in a dispute between her and Tunisia, the popular reaction was so great as to bring down the government and to lead to a greater crisis which ultimately led to the disappearance of the Fourth Republic and the installation of de Gaullė in power.

This case is singularly important as it shows that even in the case of a great power, proud of its traditions, importance and prestige, military alliance inevitably brings in its train political influence. It failed in the case of France because, in spite of her apparent political instability, French people were united enough and the alliance was far from being one-sided. But experience elsewhere, especially in Asian countries, bears witness to the internal dangers of such alliances. In the case of India, the situation might not be so dangerous as to affect the political independence, but her own experience in the past has emphasized the lesson which history has taught, that an alliance of unequal states is dangerous to the freedom of the weaker partner.

Also, if a country depends too heavily on foreign alliances for its defence, it is likely to shirk the heavy sacrifices necessary to develop its own strength. When India thinks of defence, she thinks not merely of training her armies or perfecting their organization, but also of industrial and economic strength and the advancement of scientific research ; in fact, the building up of the total strength of the nation in order to be able to withstand external attacks. This means not only a determination to defend her freedom but to accept continuous and heavy sacrifices in order to be able to do so. If on the other hand, she begins to depend upon external help, and places her trust more in alliances than in her own efforts, the almost certain result would be a weakening of her efforts to stand on her own feet.

Further, an unequal alliance of this nature creates social and political strains within the community which lead to instability. It creates vested interests, allied with outsiders who come to exercise dominant political power leading to rivalries and conflicts. A weak country incapable of defending itself without foreign support is *ex hypothesi* a backward country in respect of its economy, industrial power, etc. These have to be propped up by external help, thus further weakening the economic and social structure of the country.

The history of every Asian country allied with great powers demonstrates this fact beyond any doubt. The case of Kuomintang China is too well known to need repetition here. After the second World War, Thailand passed into the American orbit and became a military ally of the United States, staunchly loyal and determined to support allied policies. America, on her part, has given Thailand every kind of support and made her the bastion of her anti-communist policies in South-East Asia. While the alliance has flourished, the internal tensions in Thailand, as a consequence of this protected independence, have been such that revolutionary dictatorships have followed one after another, and the political life of the country has shown the peculiar characteristic of the army being ranged against the navy. Pakistan is another Asian country where the confusion reached such a stage that the military had to take over and abrogate the constitution. An American analyst, Mr. Rivkin, has even gone to the extent of saying that American financial support to defence has " generally resulted in the enhancement of the military as a focus of power, prestige and stability in the presence of general political instability and economic stagnation", and he frankly declares that, " the part that external military assistance plays in raising the status of military leaders should cause us to question the responsibility we bear for political developments". In fact, anyone who studies the internal tensions — economic, social and political — created by depending too heavily on foreign assistance in the matter of defence will see clearly that the decision of India to remain outside alliances and groupings, and to develop her own defensive strength has not only been wise, but is the only one suited to her conditions.

This, of course, does not mean that in case she is actually attacked she would not accept assistance from others. No country has ever held such a view. Faced with Nazi aggression, Britain and France bid for Soviet support. When Hitler attacked the Soviet Union, Moscow welcomed the help of America and the Western allies. That is different from basing one's defence policy on support from stronger powers, or taking shelter behind the strength of others.

The conditions of India's defence today are, as we have tried to emphasize, different from what they were under the British. During the British period there was no direct threat to India's borders. It is true that the Soviet Union's borders came near to those of undivided India on the Pamirs. But the threat across that area was negligible. Otherwise, India's neighbours were practically powerless in relation to the strength of the British in India. The last ten years, however, have witnessed the growth of new areas of sensitivity. As we have seen, the partition created for India two unnatural boundaries, one in the east and the other in the west. Both these boundaries create special problems. Again, from the Karakoram in Central Asia to the Lushai ranges on the borders of Burma, the whole of the Himalayan boundary has become a sensitive area for defence. With Tibet organized under the Chinese, India's northern boundary across the Himalayas also becomes a sensitive border, which has to be watched and protected.

Recent events have emphasized the significance of this change. The armed forces of the Chinese Peoples' Republic having reached the Indian border, on the Indian side also the military has had to take control. In the outer region of Ladakh, over mountain peaks where snow never melts and in areas swept by the ice-cold winds, with but sparse population in a few sheltered valleys, in scattered patches of pasture land where cattle from both sides feed at certain times, on the border lands of Sikkim and Bhutan and along the high ranges marked by the McMahon line, both sides have become active in patrolling, in the creation of check posts, in the building of strategic communication and other normal precautions of defence. Incidents like the occupation of Longju have excited the public mind. Though the danger of a serious invasion of India's territory or a penetration into the Indian plains from across the Tibetan highlands and the high Himalayan ranges is no more than a chimera, the danger of the unsettlement of the border population and a threat to strategic areas have created a new awareness of defence problems in public mind and helped to develop in Indian mind a frontier-complex, the absence of which had helped foreign invaders in the past.

Apart from the land frontiers, India's extensive coast-line has also become a matter to be considered seriously from the point of view of defence. Britain, it is true, maintains her bases in the Indian Ocean, at Singapore and at Aden and no doubt in due course she will develop a powerful base on the African coast. That may help to prevent the entry of other nations into the Arabian Sea to threaten the coasts of India. But how far, in case of a crisis in Europe itself, Britain will be able to maintain a fleet powerful enough to fulfil these functions in the Indian Ocean is a matter of doubt. It should be remembered that in the second World War she was not able to do so at certain periods. It was then that India was most exposed to danger. That situation may well arise again and may constitute a greater threat to India's security than any invasion from the side of the land, either from the north or through the traditional route of invasions in the north-west. For an invasion across the land frontiers, the obstacles are formidable. An invasion of North India is no doubt possible across her land frontiers, but the conquest of India would require a sustained military effort across long distances, through difficult passes and under trying climatic conditions. If India's unity holds and she is led with even ordinary competence, an invasion from the land side presents no serious threat to Indian independence. But the position is different in the case of an attack from the side of the sea. If the mastery of the Indian seas is established by a hostile power, its pressure could be relentless, since India's economic life is dependent on maritime trade. An overwhelming percentage of her trade is carried in ships through the sea lanes of the Indian Ocean. Attack from the sea is more dangerous to the freedom of India than any threat from across her land frontiers.

So long, however, as the country is united and landpower is well organized, a conquest from the seaside is never a serious possibility. India withstood superior naval power for nearly three hundred years, from 1498 to 1765, and it was only when the central government in India broke down in the second half of the eighteenth century that the powers based on the sea began to think seriously in terms of conquest. But that does not rule out the possibility of naval powers continuously exercising pressure to gain their political objectives, if India remains weak on the sea and is not organized to meet that threat. Though the days of wanton bombardments and "pacific blockades" may be said to be over, there are instances even in recent times which should warn us that in times of crisis, great states enjoying world-wide power through their navies will not hesitate to weaken the internal structure of countries by enforcing what may amount to a blockade.

Viewed from all these angles, it will be seen that India's fundamental problem in respect of her defence is the development of her industrial strength, based on continuous progress in scientific research. It is impossible in modern times to achieve industrial strength without a satisfactory and continued progress in science, keeping the country abreast of others in this all-important field. Any dependence on second-hand science would only mean second class arms and equipment, outmoded even before the defence forces have mastered their use. This we see today in respect of our air force. By the time we have acquired for our air force machines which are considered up-to-date and effective, other and better types are reaching the production lines. So in the present circumstances the Indian air force, however well-trained and competent, cannot catch up with the air force of a scientifically advanced country. This, of course, is well recognized by her defence planners, who realize that purchase of planes abroad and even production in the country under licence, can but help to bridge the gulf between our own production based on independent research and total dependence on others.

It is not difficult to develop defence industries unrelated to the general standard of industrial growth. Some countries have been forced to adopt such a programme as a result of international pressure. The Soviet Union's first three plans concentrated heavily on industries, which had a direct relation to defence potential to the neglect, it is now recognized, of consumer goods. Poland also, before the tragic events of Poznan had followed a similar line. But such a policy is not possible in the circumstances of India in view of the appalling poverty of the masses, the inadequacy of food production and the generally colonial character of the economy that she inherited from the British. The basic requirement of India is for a general economic advance without neglecting her defence needs and it is on that she is concentrating. When her scientific work has advanced sufficiently and her industry is expanded enough to take advantage of it, her problem of defence would have been solved. Till that time it will always be a question of following well behind what the more advanced countries are doing.

Though this is not by any means an ideal position to be in, it cannot be considered unsatisfactory in regard to the states of her region. None of her neighbours, not even China, is in a position of self-sufficiency in regard to defence. The basic situation in respect of all the countries of the region is that effective defence organization is dependent upon the growth of a self-developing industrial system based on a high level of scientific research. The only serious military power, outside the Soviet Union, in this area, which both by her size and the efforts which she is making to catch up in the sphere of industry and science is China. The high plateau of Tibet and the almost impenetrable snow-clad Himalayan ranges lie between the centre of dynamic power in China and the Gangetic valley, and any serious threat to India's safety could well be discounted. This does not mean that India's Himalayan frontiers will be peaceful as in former times.

The other neighbouring areas pose no immediate threat. There are many in India, who, looking back on the past, consider that a major threat to India exists, at least potentially, in the Islamic power which stretches from Morocco to Lahore. But a moment's consideration would show that this is no more than the fear of a historical ghost. The threat from across the Khyber and Bolan passes loomed large only when the internal structure of India had broken down; and simultaneously the states of the area from which the attack came represented an advance in military technique. At all times when India's central organization was strong from the period of the Mauryas to that of the British, the threat from across the Indus was not militarily serious. Today the position is altogether different. Offensive power is based on technological advancement and in this respect the Islamic world presents no threat to India.

The basic questions in respect of India's defence therefore are, whether the unity and integration that India has achieved will last, and whether her present efforts to modernize herself through industrialization and scientific advancement will succeed. If the fissiparous tendencies now under effective control assert themselves, or her unity breaks down through other causes, then the problem of India's defence will become serious. Equally, if India in spite of her efforts fails to achieve a self-generating industrial growth or her bid for scientific progress or technological advancement breaks down through weakness of national effort, then the problem of her defence would present other and almost insuperable difficulties. The awareness of this fact is the greatest security for India's defence.

INDEX